Monty Python

A CELEBRATION

Monty Python

A CELEBRATION

RICHARD TOPPING

with additional material by
Chris Long

Virgin

To Katie. Thank you.

Acknowledgements: My biggest debt of gratitude goes to friend and fellow Python fan Chris Long, whose hard work on researching the TV shows made sure this book was completed. And to all those who leant me videos, books and records... thank you. You'll get them back, eventually.

First published in Great Britain in 1999 by
Virgin Publishing Limited
Thames Wharf Studios
Rainville Road
London W6 9HT

A catalogue record for this book is available from the British Library

ISBN 1 85227 825 0

Photos: Pictorial Press; Camera Press; MSI; London Features; Hulton Getty; Popperfoto; Topham Picture Library; Kobal; Rex Features; Ronald Grant; All Action; Kettledrum, BBC, Rediffusion, Python/courtesy of Aquarius Library; Columbia/courtesy of Pictorial Press.

Designed by Design 23, London.
Printed and bound by WBC Book Manufacturers, Bridgend, Mid Glam.

Contents

Cleese, Palin, Chapman, Idle, Gilliam and Jones in October 1969, when the first series was broadcast.

The birth of Monty Python's Flying Circus

and a machine that goes 'ping'

In October 1998, the *Sun* newspaper ran a full front-page story on what it considered to be the demise of the Tory Party. The page consisted of a picture of a parrot, hanging upside down on its perch, with the head of William Hague, the leader of the opposition, superimposed on to its feathery shoulders. The headline alongside read 'IT IS AN EX-PARTY'.

It was, of course, a reference to a television comedy sketch, possibly the most famous ever made – *Monty Python*'s Dead Parrot. That a thirty-year-old comedy act should be famous enough to be used as a cultural reference in a newspaper headline is astonishing. But then *Monty Python* was – in every sense – an astonishing phenomenon, not simply changing the comedy of its day, but influencing and inspiring generation after generation of comics since it first appeared on British television in 1969.

It's difficult now to imagine a world without *Monty Python's Flying Circus*. No Knights Who Say Ni, no Ex-Parrots, no Nudge Nudge, Wink Wink. From the surreal visuals and the clever wordplays to the cruel caricatures and the sheer stupidity of it all, *Python* has become a bedrock of our shared consciousness. But above all, it was funny – side-splittingly, tear-inducingly, pant-wettingly *funny*.

It was being so funny that gave rise to a curious aspect of the *Python* legacy, The-Day-After-The-Show-Was-Broadcast-Public-Recitals. Starting with *The Goons* in the 50s, comedy fans would gather in small groups and repeat their favourite lines in hushed and reverential tones. But *Python* took this to new limits. From student-union bars and sixth-form common rooms, to the coffee machine at the office and the locker room at the squash club, *Python* bolstered the 'repeating your favourite catchphrases in front of your mates' syndrome to unbelievable heights. How many times have you professed yourself too full to eat another mouthful when some wag says 'Just one waf-ur theen meent, monsieur'; or been irritating a friend to be told that 'your father ees a hamster and yur mother smells of elderberries'? This sense of mass involvement in comedy means there's a bit of *Python* in everyone, a shared comedic experience that we all refer to, whether we're fans of *Monty Python* or not.

Yet it's strange to think that this outstanding comedic legacy started with six young men gathered in an Indian restaurant in Hampstead with no clear idea what they were trying to do, and a BBC budget that needed spending. And that, from such inauspicious beginnings, they went on to make four television series, four major movies, numerous live shows, records, books and (individually) some of the greatest comedy and drama of their generation.

So how did it all come about?

THE FAMILY HISTORY

John Cleese has long argued that no comedy is truly original; it is all, in one way or another, derivative of its predecessors, growing and mutating in much the same way that popular music does. In one sense, he is right – *Monty Python* can trace its true roots back to when the individual members were boys, listening to the crazy,

unpredictable and downright silly humour of *The Goon Show* on their radio in the 50s. But in another sense Cleese is wrong, because in his analysis there are no major evolutionary leaps, merely a succession of slowly changing and self-feeding influences. But, occasionally, something comes along that climbs four rungs up the evolutionary ladder instead of the customary one, or (to really push the analogy to the limits) leaps off its own and starts climbing up a completely different ladder. Actually, maybe it's not a ladder; maybe it's a flight of stairs. Well, two flights of stairs next to each other. Oh anyway …

It's often forgotten that *Monty Python* was a product of the 60s – of flower power, miniskirts, The Beatles and LSD. This was a creative and liberating time – sexually, politically and socially the entire landscape of society was being changed, and nowhere was this more reflected than in the comedy of the day. But the foundations of this

John Cleese, Marty Feldman, Aimi Macdonald, Graham Chapman and Tim Brooke-Taylor in At Last The 1948 Show.

change had first been laid in the 50s, when the world was at long last recovering from the shock of the Second World War. The 50s signalled the end of rationing, the first broadcasts from ITV, the explosion of rock and roll. They marked the beginnings of a true 'youth culture', and with it a growing mistrust and lack of respect for 'the Establishment': royalty, parliament, the civil service, the Church, the judiciary, the armed services, the public schools and authority figures of all kinds. This dissolution of respect found a focal point in comedy, and nowhere was this youthful irreverence more focused than in the Footlights Club of Cambridge University.

The Cambridge University Footlights Club was established in 1883, and was from its very outset a vehicle for light-hearted musical comedy. But it was never cutting-edge or innovative – its material usually consisted of amusing ditties or cheery playlets. All that was to change in the late 50s, when a surge of creative talent entered the university and altered the entire culture of the club. Up until then, there was no tradition of doing 'something different' with the revues each year, no agenda for radicalism. But, with the arrival of people like Jonathan Miller, Alan Bennett and John Bird, that soon changed. The revues become more satirical, more political, and, most importantly, more innovative. With the addition of Dudley Moore and Peter Cook, the club's transformation was complete, and a new and dangerous style of comedy was emerging. It was a style that embraced change, that made fun of authority figures, that found humour in the mundane as well as the magnificent.

First enjoying success in John Bird's groundbreaking 1959 revue *The Last Laugh*, and then emerging later as *Beyond the Fringe*, these five young men took the

David Frost cracks a joke: John Cleese and Ronnie Corbett remember he's the boss. (The Frost Report).

unique Cambridge brand of humour down to London in 1960. There it played to packed houses, seeding ideas to a whole new generation of potential comics.

It was with this tide of change that a fresh wave of talent crashed on to Cambridge: David Frost, Graeme Gardner, Bill Oddie, John Cleese, Tim Brooke-Taylor, Graham Chapman, Eric Idle and many, many more entered the Footlights and picked up where Cook and Co. had left off. Meanwhile, at Oxford University, Cambridge's sister campus, a similar process was taking place, with young men such as Terry Jones and Michael Palin starting their own revue clubs and inventing new and exciting styles of comedy.

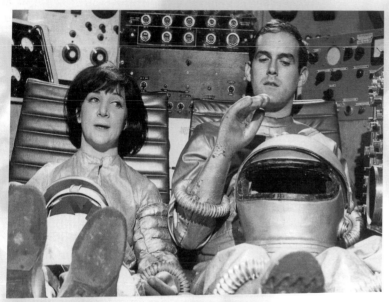

Sheila Steafel and John Cleese get a bit spacey in The Frost Report.

By the early 1960s both sets of performers were appearing at the increasingly popular Edinburgh Festival, where they met and cross-fertilised their ideas. The Cambridge crowd had a notable success with their 1964 *Clump of Plinths* revue, which went on to West End success as *Cambridge Circus*; while the Oxford men had finished their degrees and been snapped up as writers and performers at the BBC. By 1965 and 1966, all of the future members of *Monty Python* were – in one way or another – writing and performing on shows that had them meeting and working together on radio, for BBC television and for ITV.

It was *The Frost Report* in 1966 that first brought them all (bar Gilliam) together under one roof, but the *Python*s-to-be were beginning to tire of the heavily satirical tone of the show, and were looking to work on other projects where the material that they really found funny would have a voice. Mixing the differing styles of the universities – Cambridge very structured and pragmatic; Oxford very 'woolly' and romantic – gave plenty of opportunity for developing their skills further. In 1969 – after all six of the *Python*s had earned themselves reputations throughout the corridors of the BBC – they were brought together by producer Barry Took to make a new and innovative comedy show.

Welcome to *Owl Stretching Time*.

IT WAS MY IDEA

There is argument even now over how the group came to be assembled. Barry Took claims it was all his idea, and that he contacted John Cleese (at that time the definite 'anchor' for the whole project) to discuss how it might be put into action. Cleese, on the other hand, claims it was his idea, and that it was he who got in touch with Took. Either way, the six men were brought together – the five university performers and a young animator whom Eric Idle had introduced to producer Humphrey Barclay a couple of years previously – for an initial meeting at the BBC which was then reconvened at a curry house in Hampstead.

Almost immediately the ideas started flowing, and many of the group resurrected sketches that had been abandoned on *The Frost Report* because they were too silly or not satirical enough. For inspiration they also started looking around at other innovative comedy, and took considerable influence from Spike Milligan's stream-of-consciousness *Q5*, which showed them that the traditional sketch format could be abandoned. You didn't *have* to have a punchline.

Barry Took wisely gave them a completely free rein, seeing how the constraints on the other shows to which they had contributed blunted their creative edge. And so over the next few months, writing in the same partnerships that had endured throughout their university and early BBC days, the *Pythons* created the first series of *Monty Python's Flying Circus*. And what a series it was. Containing some of the most enduring *Python* sketches of all time, it was an assault of comedic talent, and from its first broadcast was instantly and rightly recognised not so much as a breath of fresh air, but as a force-ten gale with lashing rain and lightning strikes.

WHAT'S IN A NAME?

The name had been a bone of contention for some time. Graham Chapman, being the only medically qualified one, said it was a femur, but Palin insisted he'd seen a similar looking one in a butcher's shop in Cheam, and that it was a collar bone. Discussions of the bone aside, the possible names are well documented:

The Amazing Flying Circus
Arthur Buzzard's Flying School
Arthur Megapode's Cheap Show
Arthur Megapode's Flying Circus
Baron Von Took's Flying Circus
Bob Python's Flying Circus
Brian's Flying Circus
The Comedy Zoo
Cynthia Fellatio's Flying Circus
The Down Show

Gwen Dibley's Flying Circus
A Spoon and a Basin
The Horrible Earnest Megapode
The Joke Zoo
The Laughing Zoo
Man's Crisis of Identity in the Latter Half
*   of the Twentieth Century*
Megapode's Cheap Show
Norman Python's Flying Circus
O

123
Ow! It's Colin Plint!
Owl Stretching Time
The Panic Show
The People Zoo

The Plastic Mac Show
Vaseline Parade
The Year of the Stoat
Zoo Show!

In the end, *Flying Circus* was chosen because it was stuffy, middle-class BBC-speak for the First World War, and Barry Took – who was seen as rather arrogant and stubborn – had acquired the nickname of Baron von Took (hence Baron Von Took's Flying Circus). *Monty Python* was chosen because the group felt it represented the name of a shady, small-time theatrical booker. Gwen Dibley – which was Palin's favourite – was a name he spotted in a Women's Institute magazine.

NAME THAT TUNE!

Monty Python had an immediate look and feel – partly Gilliam's animation, partly the music, and partly the new style of sketch that the *Pythons* were popularising. But, to fans the world over, it is the opening credits that say everything that needs to be said about *Monty Python's Flying Circus*, and for that we have to thank Terry Gilliam.

The theme music to *Monty Python's Flying Circus* is Sousa's *Liberty Bell*, chosen by Palin and Gilliam. Gilliam loved it because it was American and reminded him of stuffy, military-band marches back home; while Palin just thought it was great. Gilliam rearranged the piece to fit into the thirty-second time slot allocated for the opening credits, and had the distinctive bong at the beginning made much louder just to make it sound more ridiculous.

The popularity of *Monty Python* has meant that this piece of music has now been widely abandoned by brass bands the world over. Nothing quite reduces the solemnity of a military march more than a song that brings to mind two grown men slapping their faces with fishes.

NO POLITICS, BUT PLENTY POLITICAL

What was the secret behind *Monty Python*? Why did it become such a hugely successful phenomenon? One answer lies in the dynamics of the group: six highly talented and creative individuals brought together with one objective – make people laugh. But the *Pythons* were never a bunch who felt bound to each other. Each had his own interests and particular skills, and as a group they did as much fighting and disagreeing with each other as they did collaborating. It has been said that on some occasions they actually quite disliked each other.

There were two major 'camps' in the group. First Cleese and Chapman, the original Footlights men, who had worked together at college and stayed as a strong writing

The Pythons *consider the punchline to the Dirty Fork sketch. Yes, it is funny.*

partnership throughout all of the *Python* projects. There were Jones and Palin, the Oxford men, who had been similarly allied since their days at university. And then there were Gilliam and Idle, who, although preferring to work alone, tended to side with Oxford and Cambridge respectively (Idle was in the Footlights a year or so after Cleese). This internal balance meant that no particular crew ever held the balance of power, and in the often heartless script meetings each person could count on a measure of support. The two camps also had vastly different styles. Chapman and Cleese were very pedantic, spending hours poring over a single line, crafting it to comedic perfection. Palin and Jones, however, were more content to pour out ideas in a woollier, less structured fashion. With Idle's bent for comic songs (plus contributions from the unofficial *Python* Neil Innes) and Gilliam's visual wizardry, the range of skills and styles was eclectic indeed. Each *Python* took inspiration from the others, and through a process of synergy, alchemy, biology, buffoonery and astrology created some of the most memorable comedy of our time.

This loose collective also meant that the *Pythons* could go away and do their own projects without threatening the sanctity of the group. In fact, their willingness to allow each other complete artistic freedom outside of *Monty Python* often meant that they developed skills that they brought back into the *Python* fold, such as Jones's burgeoning directorial talents and Gilliam's unique eye for design. And by giving themselves time off, a break from each other, they could come back to each new *Python* project with a fresh outlook.

But let's not forget where it all started. Sunday 5 October 1969, with the broadcast of the first ever *Monty Python's Flying Circus* on BBC1, in a slot usually reserved for religious programmes.

Although it initially met them with a resounding silence, the world would never be the same again.

Monty Python's Flying Circus

From *the first* TV show in 1969 to the last in 1979, the BBC produced a total of 45 half-hour episodes on *Monty Python's Flying Circus* (actually, not entirely true as the last series was simply entitled *Monty Python*, but you get the idea). Each episode contained about six to ten sketches. If you've done the maths in your head, you've probably already worked out that, with about 300 – 400 *Python* sketches, sadly there is not enough room in this book to mention each and every one of them. Indeed, there's barely enough room to mention each episode. In fact, you're lucky I'm even mentioning the TV shows at all, given how expensive it is to make books these days.

The long and short of it is that I have tried to cover as many favourites as possible without missing out the really important ones, while saying as much as I can about the series themselves in order to put the development of *Monty Python* into context. Since Series One and Two were generally superior, they get most of the airtime. This means – inevitably – that some people's favourite sketches won't get mentioned.

If you have any complaints, send your letters to:

'Hi'm harresting you on a charge of makin' silly sketches.'

I Really Don't Agree With Your
  Choice of Sketches Very Much
The Skip Out Front Full of Kitchen Rubbish
Virgin Publishing
Fulham
London

It's···

I shall, of course, completely ignore them.

Series One

It's a pretty obvious thing to say, but here goes anyway – *Monty Python* started with the TV shows, first broadcast on 5 October 1969. In all the years since then, after all the films, the records, the books and the stage shows, it's easy to forget that something so significant should begin with a humble television sketch show.

Even though the team developed their special skills individually and in small groups, it was only when given the freedom to work together with the full resources of the BBC behind them that things crystallised and *Monty Python's Flying Circus* became the jewel in the crown of British TV comedy. Once Barry Took got them together he took the very sensible step of standing back and letting the *Python*s get their act(s) together – stepping in only to help in various skirmishes with BBC management (of which there were plenty).

In the first couple of series the shows develop almost exponentially; the first series is a masterpiece of comic writing, and arguably the best, but it is interesting to watch how the individual performances and the use of television as a medium develops. All of the team – bar Gilliam – had previous TV experience, but not with this degree of freedom or with this kind of material. It would be wrong to say they invented this style of television (Spike Milligan had been doing similar stuff for a while with his seminal *Q5*), but they refined the technique and, more importantly, made it accessible and funny – something that Milligan occasionally failed to do.

It is clear that, by about the middle of Series One, all of the players are more relaxed with both the *Python* format and the novelty of having to perform their own material in a TV studio. By the end of this series the *Python*s

Initial reaction to Monty Python's Flying Circus *was muted indeed, leaving the* Python*s up the creek with only three paddles.*

had even taken to using the studio as part of their jokes, something they refined for the live tour, when Cleese and Idle would often be seen trawling the audience.

One curious fact is that the BBC – for reasons best known to themselves – decided to change the order of broadcast, so that the show that was recorded first was actually broadcast second. There doesn't appear to have been any quality issue – both shows are (of course) absolutely superb, but it gives an interesting insight into how the BBC perceived the whole *Python* thing: they just didn't *get* it.

Terry Gilliam, the 'stand-alone' performer, is worth a mention, because his material seems not to change very much in the first series; his animations start brilliantly and continue that brilliance throughout the thirteen shows. His job was slightly more difficult than the rest simply because he usually completed his animations on his own and delivered them finished to the group – often on the day of the studio shoot.

It is bordering on the tedious to explain yet again just how good these shows were, but it needs to be said simply to appreciate the power of the writing and the ideas behind them. Show One, Series One – despite being the second recorded – contains one of the most enduring names from *Monty Python*: Arthur 'Two Sheds' Jackson. But Jackson was just one of many *Python* classics that sprung from that first creative outpouring, and it is astonishing just how many of the most memorable *Python* characters come from the first part of the first series.

THE FORMAT

While many of us remember the characters from *Python*, we tend to forget how the show helped change the form of British TV. The beginning of all of the shows in Series One consisted of a dishevelled character played by Michael Palin (the 'It's Man' or 'Hermit'), who runs towards the camera and eventually says 'it's', so kicking off Gilliam's opening animations and the theme music. In Show One the 'It's Man' takes a full fifty seconds to get from the sea, over the beach and across the sand dunes to the camera before he says his word (shot on a Bournemouth beach, incidentally). What a tragedy it would have been for Palin if he'd ever forgotten his line...

In other words, an expectant and unassuming audience had to wait almost an entire minute before it heard a peep from 'this new *Monty Python* lot everyone's been talking about'. It may not seem too significant now, but this was 1969 and British TV was simply not done like this.

In the States, TV programmes were structured rather differently from their British counterparts. There, viewers would often get a 'teaser' – a couple of minutes of action before the opening titles – that was designed to grab the attention and 'tease' the viewer into watching the rest of the show. No such thing at the BBC, which at the time was editing its American imports so that the first thing the viewer saw was the opening titles, then the teaser. Right from the word 'it's', *Python* was breaking the TV mould.

Series One Show One – 'Whither Canada?'

Recorded as Show Two on 7 September 69

Transmitted on 5 October 69

'It's Wolfgang Amadeus Mozart'; Famous Deaths; Italian Lesson; Whizzo Butter; 'It's the Arts'; Arthur 'Two Sheds' Jackson; Picasso/Cycling Race; The Funniest Joke in the World.

For no apparent reason the first show was subtitled 'Whither Canada?'. This was one of the rejected names for the series – of which there were hundreds. Most of the other shows in this series had a subtitle, but only one of them, 'Owl Stretching Time', was also known to be a rejected series name.

In this show was the Funniest Joke in the World, a cod Second World War documentary about the writing of a joke that made people laugh so hard they died, and its subsequent use in the defeat of the Germans. It is an interesting – typically *Python* – sketch because of its sophisticated manipulation of the time line. It starts in the present day (the 1960s) and then without missing a beat and without any explanation moves back to the Second World War. An unusual trick well handled and one that shows us how the *Python*s made little concession to their audience – you either kept up with their ideas or you didn't bother watching.

In the first series each show had a theme running through it – pigs, teeth and sheep being some of the favourites. Thus the first sketch of the first show is number one in a series of pig references that occur throughout, finishing at the end of the show with the statement: 'Pigs 9 British Bipeds 4. The pigs go on to meet Vicky Carr in the final.' To those watching, it was immediately apparent that this was no ordinary comedy.

To 'The Establishment' the Python*s were just another bunch of layabouts.*

Series One Show Two – 'Sex and Violence'

Recorded as Show One on 30 August 69

Transmitted on 12 October 69

Flying Sheep; French Lecture on Sheep Aircraft; A Man With Three Buttocks; A Man With Two Noses; Musical Mice; Marriage Guidance Counsellor; The Wacky Queen; Working-Class Playwright; A Scotsman on a Horse; The Wrestling Epilogue; The Mouse Problem.

Show Two is the first time we hear the phrase 'And now for something completely different' (delivered by Eric Idle), as well as being the first time we see the black and white film of the little old ladies clapping. Two of the main images we associate with *Monty Python's Flying Circus* were in the first show ever recorded.

The second show (the first ever recorded) has a shorter run for the 'It's Man', and kicks off with the Sheep sketch, which includes the classic phrase 'He's that most dangerous of animals – a clever sheep'. Despite the fact that the players look vaguely uncomfortable on television, there is no sense of learning on the job here, no feeling of them being unsure of what they wanted to achieve. *Python* hit the screen fully formed.

Next up is the French Lecture on Sheep Aircraft. This is the first time we see Michael Palin – who of all the *Python*s was the most prone to getting the giggles – laughing in the middle of the sketch as he hands over the false moustache to John Cleese.

Eric Idle as the marriage guidance counsellor seduces Palin's wife.

Series One Show Three – 'How to Recognise Different Types of Tree From Quite a Long Way Away'

Recorded as Show Three on 14 September 69
Transmitted on 19 October 69
Court Scene (witness in coffin/Cardinal Richelieu); The Larch; Bicycle Repair Man; Children's Stories; Restaurant Sketch; Seduced Milkman; Stolen Newsreader; Children's Interview; Nudge Nudge.

Show Three saw a development of the 'It's Man' idea, as Palin legs it out of the jungle chased by a lion – proof again, if proof were needed, that all things in *Python* were up for reappraisal. Nothing was ever taken for granted. It also has the immortal Nudge Nudge sketch ('Is your wife a goer?') between Eric Idle and Terry Jones. This was a typical bit of class writing from Eric Idle, who created here one of his most enduring characters (with the exception of The Parrot sketch, it was the Nudge Nudge man who used to get the best standing ovations at the live concerts, even before Idle had said a word). This show's running theme is trees ('Number one, the Larch').

In a turn for the worse for Palin's 'It's Man', the lion savages him in the end credits (by all accounts, a very painful place to get savaged).

Series One Show Four – 'Owl Stretching Time'

Recorded as Show Four on 21 September 69

Transmitted on 26 October 69

Song (And Did Those Teeth …); Art Gallery; Art Critic; It's a Man's Life in the Modern Army; Undressing in Public; Self-Defence; Secret-Service Dentist.

The 'It's Man''s role is developed further in the introduction to Show Four, where he is thrown down a cliff at the start of the show and then crawls to the camera to say (33 seconds later) 'it's'.

The show starts with 'Did those teeth in ancients times walk upon England's mountains green …' sung by Eric Idle, so introducing the show's theme of dentistry. It is the first appearance of the Colonel – played by Graham Chapman – the bombastic military man who takes over the director's job and tells the cameras to cut to a different picture, in this case Terry Gilliam dressed as a Viking in one of his first appearances on the show.

Series One Show Five – 'Man's Crisis of Identity in the Latter Half of the Twentieth Century'

Recorded as Show Five on 3 October 69

Transmitted on 23 November 69

Confuse a Cat; The Smuggler; A Duck, a Cat and a Lizard (discussion); Vox Pops on Smuggling; Police Raid; Letters Vox Pops; Newsreader Arrested; Erotic Film; Silly Job Interview; Careers Advisory Board; Burglar/Encyclopaedia Salesman.

Show Five sees the arrival of the Gumby character, a visual mainstay of *Python* in both character and cartoon form. Although not actually called Gumby, the character is John Cleese, trousers rolled, wearing wellington boots and with a knotted handkerchief on his head, explaining in a loud voice that anyone who goes abroad shouldn't be let back into the country. It would take a little while, but this comic invention – along with the pepperpots, the *Pythons*' name for women with high-pitched voices played by the team – would become staple characters of the show.

There was a sea change on the production side from Show Five onward. This was the first show produced by Ian MacNaughton, who had worked with Spike Milligan on his *Q* series of TV shows. MacNaughton hadn't been available to produce the show from the start and was only able to direct the film inserts. In the meantime John Howard Davis had stepped in as producer. For Show Five, MacNaughton and Howard Davis swapped jobs, allowing Howard Davis to direct the rather long and truly surreal Confuse a Cat film. MacNaughton went on to produce every show from here on in.

Series One Show Six – 'An Irving C Saltzberg Production'

Recorded as Show Seven on 5 November 69

Transmitted on 30 November 69

It's the Arts; Johann Gombolputty … Von Hautkopft of Ulm; Non-Illegal Robbery; Vox Pops; Crunchy Frog; The Dull Life of a City Stockbroker; Red Indian in Theatre; Policemen Make Wonderful Friends; A Scotsman on a Horse; Twentieth-Century Vole.

Show Six was the programme with the composer that no one talks about. To talk about him would mean mentioning his name, and to mention his name is a sure-fire way to waste years of your life. Yes, it was … (deep breath) Johann Gambolputty de von Ausfern-Schplenden-Schlitter-Crasscrenbon-Fried-Digger-Dingle-Dangle-Dongle-Dungle-Burstein-Von-Knacker-Thrasher-Apple-Banger-Horowitz-Ticolensic-Grander-Knotty-Spelltinkle-Grandlich-Grumblemeyer-Spelterwasser-Kurstlich-Himbleeisen-Bahnwagen-Gutenabend-Bitte-Ein-Nurnburger-Bratwustle-Gerspurten-Mitz-Weimache-Luber-Hundsfut-Gumberaber-Shönendanker-Kalbsfleisch-Weimache-Aucher von Hautkopft of Ulm. You know you're with a heavy-duty *Python* fan when they can recite that one (try typing it).

And for chocolate connoisseurs we also get the Crunchy Frog sketch – chocolates made with real frogs (and bones) and larks' vomit. Here we can see the 'talking to the audience' method of finishing sketches begin to take off, as characters just walk on and move the show forward by simply halting the sketch and starting another. This proved to be a great liberator for the *Python*s because – like in Milligan's shows – it meant that sketches became viable when they didn't have a punchline.

Series One Show Seven – 'You're No Fun Any More'

Recorded as Show Six on 10 October 69

Transmitted on 7 December 69

Camel Spotter; You're No Fun Any More; The Audit; Science Fiction Sketch; Man Turns into Scotsman; Police Station; Blancmanges Playing Tennis.

Show Seven gives us the catchphrase 'You're no fun any more' and an incredibly long sketch about people turning into Scotsmen. And that's about it.

This show is interesting as it is generally seen as the failure of the series. The B-film approach to the aliens turning people into Scotsmen is one of the first attempts to devote a lot of the show to one idea; the result is at best rather hit and miss.

Series One Show Eight – 'Full-Frontal Nudity'

Recorded as Show Eight on 25 November 69
Transmitted on 14 December 69
Army Protection Racket; Vox Pops; Art Critic: The Place of the Nude; Buying a Bed; Hermits; Dead Parrot; The Flasher; Hell's Grannies.

Show Eight moves up a gear with several inspired – if not classic – sketches, and one, well, entirely classic sketch (more on that in a moment). Perhaps the subtle change in the show comes from two factors: first, Ian MacNaughton is by now well and truly established as producer; and second, the shows are now being broadcast. That they were being viewed by the real audience was an important landmark – it meant the team could not only see what the shows looked like in someone's front room, but they could get genuine feedback on what worked and what didn't.

One of the more inspired sketches in this show is Buying a Bed ('Someone said mattress to Mr Lambert') and yet another rendition of 'Jerusalem'. We also see the introduction and development of several characters we will meet later, notably the Vercotti Brothers (Dino Terry Jones and Luigi Michael Palin). The two of them turn up again, but more often than not Palin reprised Luigi whenever a spiv was called for.

Also in Show Eight are two effeminate hermits (played by Eric Idle and Michael Palin). This is the first time we see these

John Cleese, learning his lines parrot fashion.

characters, but they reappear later in a different guise – as judges. Their sketch is broken up by Chapman's Colonel, who is now developing into a much bigger and important character. He is now talking directly to the audience, wandering around stopping sketches that he thinks are silly. The *Python* team had discovered another

As the Colonel, Chapman may have been in a military uniform, but it's all too easy to see him as a caricature of the stuffed-shirts at the BBC who still couldn't quite get their heads round *Monty Python*. Being silly just wasn't what the BBC was all about …

Cleese, disguised as Chapman's outraged Colonel.

simple way to get in and out of sketches they felt they couldn't develop any more.

The show ends with another near classic: Hell's Grannies ('These layabouts in lace'), which develops even further into a brief sketch about Eric Idle being attacked by 'vicious gangs of keep-left signs'.

But Show Eight has to be remembered as the show that brought us the phrase 'This parrot's dead' (which is never actually said in the sketch). Written by John Cleese and Graham Chapman, the sketch actually stars Cleese and Palin (and a dead, stuffed Norwegian blue). The sketch lives on (and on and on and on and on and on and on and on and on and on) and has even become the subject of sketches itself. It really is the team at the peak of their game, and probably the most oft-quoted sketch of all time.

Series One Show Nine – 'The Ant: An Introduction'
Recorded as Show Ten on 7 December 69
Transmitted on 21 December 69
Llamas; A Man With a Tape Recorder up His Nose; Kilimanjaro Expedition (double vision); A Man With a Tape Recorder up His Brother's Nose; Homicidal Barber; Lumberjack Song; Gumby Crooner; The Refreshment Room at Bletchley; Hunting Film; The Visitors.

Show Nine is worth a mention as the first show with John Cleese wearing a dinner suit and bow tie sitting behind a BBC microphone saying 'And now for something completely different'. It's also notable for the team's growing confidence as they start using technical TV gags – first in the John Cleese and Eric Idle sketch about mountaineering where we see two Cleeses on screen. (This sketch is a rarity as Cleese and Idle hardly ever wrote together – there is only one other they wrote which appeared in Series Two.) It also has a rather bizarre link – on film – with two John Cleeses saying 'And now for something completely different'. Having not said it for eight shows they were going to squeeze everything out of it from here on in.

In this show we get the first mention of Mr Gumby (Prof. RJ Gumby), this time Graham Chapman with the knotted hankie on his head. Interestingly we don't get the full-on Gumby voice. In this incarnation, Chapman sounds a bit like Alf Garnett (which given his popularity at the time is likely to be at least part of the Gumby character).

Show Eight may have had the Parrot sketch, but Show Nine almost goes one better with the line 'I didn't want to be a barber anyway. I wanted to be a lumberjack.'

What is often forgotten about the Lumberjack Song is the terrific sketch that leads into it. In it a blood-caked Palin screams hysterically about how much he hates being a barber. And if you're really awake when you watch, you'll hear the voice on the tape recorder used at the end of the sketch continue after Palin has switched it off – highlighting that these shows didn't have much time for sketches to be done again or 'tidied up' in an edit afterwards. In fact, each show had only ninety minutes of studio time to get everything done. And, as any producer will tell you, ninety minutes is not a lot of time to produce a thirty-minute TV show.

Which of course introduces the 'Lumberjack Song' – another *Python* classic – where Michael Palin and the Fred Tomlinson Singers (augmented by Cleese and Chapman) sing about lumberjacks pressing wild flowers, wearing 'suspendies' and a bra. Playing Palin's girlfriend in the song is Connie Booth (who at the time was going out with John Cleese). It is worth noting that the last line of the song in the show was 'I wish I'd been a girlie just like my dear mama'. It has now changed over time to 'I wish I'd been a girlie just like my dear papa'.

Series One Show Ten

Recorded as Show Nine on 30 November 69

Transmitted on 28 December 69

Walk-On Part in Sketch; Bank Robber (lingerie shop); Trailer; Arthur Tree; Vocational Guidance Counsellor (chartered accountant); The First Man to Jump the Channel; Tunnelling From Godalming to Java; Pet Conversions; Gorilla Librarian; Letters to Daily Mirror; Strangers in the Night.

Given *the brilliance* of the previous programmes, Show Ten has a tough act to follow (ironic seeing as it was actually recorded in between the two). But, if there was ever an undiscovered classic that deserves more credit, it's the Vocational Guidance Counsellor, which has Palin's nobody character (later Arthur Putey) as an accountant who wants to change jobs – to a lion tamer. As proof of its pedigree, it sports the immortal line (referring to Palin's lion tamer's hat) 'It lights up and says lion tamer in big neon letters, so that you can tame them after dark when they are less stroppy'. And the sheer joy of Palin's face when he discovers he's confused lions with anteaters ...

We also get the second appearance of Palin's Luigi Vercotti (this time without the Italian accent) as the ruthless manager of Ron Obvious, the first man to attempt to jump the English Channel.

Series One Show Eleven

Recorded as Show Eleven on 14 December 69

Transmitted on 4 January 70

Letter (lavatorial humour); Interruptions; Agatha Christie; Literary Football Discussion; Undertaker's Film; Interesting People; Eighteenth-Century Social Legislation; The Battle of Trafalgar; Batley Townswomen's Guild Presents the Battle of Pearl Harbour; Undertaker's Film.

Series One Show Twelve

Recorded as Show Twelve on 21 December 69

Transmitted on 11 January 70

Falling From Building; Spectrum: Talking About Things; Visitors From Coventry; Mr Hilter; The Minehead By-Election; Police Station (silly voices); Upper-Class Twit of the Year; Ken Shabby; How Far Can a Minster Fall?

Series One Show Thirteen

Recorded as Show Thirteen on 4 January 70

Transmitted on 18 January 70

Intermissions; Restaurant (abuse/cannibalism); Advertisements; Albatross; Come Back to My Place; Me Doctor; Historical Impersonations Quiz Programme; 'Probe-Around' on Crime; Stonehenge; Mr Attila the Hun; Psychiatry: Silly Sketch; Operating Theatre (squatters).

The last of the series hints at the *Pythons*' growing obsession with deconstructing the form of the TV show: immediately after the 'It's Man' says his word an INTERMISSION caption is put up and then the opening credits roll. And as a harbinger of things to come, we see Terry Jones with hardly any clothes on. The minor classics in this show are the Albatross sketch ('What flavour is it?' – 'It's bloody seabird flavour, isn't it') and the Me Doctor sketch ('Me doctor; you nurse'). But you can't escape the end-of-term feel, as the sketches are started and stopped for no apparent reason.

One of the characters in the final sketch of the series is called Mr Notlob – a direct reference to the Parrot sketch, where it is suggested that the palindrome of 'Bolton' is 'Notlob' (Bolton backwards).

This feeling quickly gives way to a touch of cynicism about the show and the BBC. One of the last pieces features an animated head saying 'What a terrible way to end a series'. And to top that, after the end credits, the intermission caption is put up again and John Cleese says: 'When this series returns it will be put out on Monday mornings as a test card, and will be described in the *Radio Times* as a history of Irish agriculture.' This reflected the frustration the team was feeling with the BBC, and was a direct reference to the cavalier way the shows were scheduled or dropped throughout the series' transmission. It was more than apparent that the BBC didn't think much of its new programme.

Pulling silly faces was an indispensible part of BBC publicity shots.

Series Two

The Minister for Silly Walks.

No matter what hindsight might suggest, the second series of *Monty Python* was not a foregone conclusion – not least because the *Python*s had an innate ability to bite the hand that was feeding them, including making many pointed jibes at the corporation in the shows. Even so, there was a positive reaction from the press and a small but vocal audience was found. And, let's face it, by most yardsticks the show was very funny – which when you're making a comedy show is about all you can hope for. So it was that a second series was commissioned, and recorded between June and October 1970. Perhaps as a result of the unease felt about *Python* in the BBC, the shows weren't scheduled to go out for nearly three months after the first show was recorded, giving the powers that be an opportunity to check the content before transmission. So it was, in true *Python* tradition, that the fourth show recorded was the first to be transmitted.

The relationship with the BBC was still strained. BBC Scotland saw fit to run the show on different nights and the various BBC regions would opt out when they had regional programming to screen. None of this helped the *Python*s' relationship with the corporation.

Series Two Show One

Recorded as Show Four on 9 July 70
Transmitted on 15 September 70
Face the Press; New Cooker; Tobacconist (prostitute advert); The Ministry of Silly Walks; The Piranha Brothers.

As to be expected, the first show has at least one classic sketch, but the beginning of the show highlights how their writing had matured in the six months between series. The show now starts with a 'And now for something completely different' from Cleese and then all but a cursory 'it's' from the 'It's Man', before the credits kick in. It was Series Two that was to make this *Monty Python* catchphrase one of the best-known lines in comedy.

The highlight of this show is The Ministry of Silly Walks, which shows Cleese's astonishing elasticity as he bends his legs into impossible shapes. Two things stand out from this sketch. First, the brilliant move from the previous sketch (The Tobacconist/Prostitute Advert sketch), an effortless change from one skit to the other, and an example of their growing understanding of television. But what is most apparent is just how much the audience understands what is going on – and loudly enjoys it.

Directly after the Silly Walks sketch we get another pointer as to how much *Python* has developed. With the phrase 'There is a choice of viewing on BBC1', *Python* struck fear into many parts of the BBC. At the time it was unheard of for a show to have the revolving-globe BBC logo in it – the logo was specifically for the bits between the shows. The continuity announcers are the people who talk between the shows, telling you what's coming up next. To have a continuity announcement – replete with the spinning-globe BBC logo – in the middle of a show (an irreverent comedy show at that) was likely to cause palpitations in the sturdiest of BBC managers. And, of course, the

John Cleeses tries to pretend they're not his friends.

The first series had all sorts of audience problems with people not understanding what was going on – giving a muted response to what we now see as classic sketches (Dead Parrot is a prime example of a sketch apparently not setting the audience alight). But the Silly Walks sketch has the audience almost in hysterics. Some lines are lost because of the laughter, and as it progresses the laughter gets louder and louder. We are no longer watching a small show of which only we are aware – this is now a wholly successful show and everyone is in on the joke.

This ending of Show Two had not been easy to achieve, and its story highlights the sorts of problems that *Python* had been getting with the BBC. To use the word 'bugger', a negotiation had been entered into whereby they had to lose a 'bloody' and a couple of 'bleedin's'. There are many stories like this, culminating in the cutting of the word 'masturbation' from a sketch, while the phrase 'strangling whippets' was allowed. Palin said that this suggested the BBC didn't mind the idea of whippets being strangled, but masturbation was clearly off the er … beaten track. Perhaps as a mark of the frustration they were all feeling, Cleese delivers the line 'I'd like to be in programme planning but I have a degree' during a sketch in the Spanish Inquisition show.

audience loved it.

Once again, *Monty Python* was breaking new ground.

The next sketch gives us the Piranha Brothers (Doug and Dinsdale) and a giant hedgehog called Spiny Norman. And as if to prove that *Python* was no longer playing by the rules, after the end credits have rolled, the show continues until Cleese's announcer appears and says good night.

Series Two Show Two

Recorded as Show Three on 2 July 70
Transmitted on 22 September 70
Man-Powered Flight; The Spanish Inquisition; Jokes and Novelties Salesman; Tax on Thingie; Vox Pops; Photos of Uncle Ted (Spanish Inquisition); The Semaphore Version of Wuthering Heights; Julius Caesar on an Aldis Lamp; Court Scene (charades).

The second show in this series has the phrase 'Trouble at mill …', which for *Python* fans everywhere is the cue for the sketch everyone expects: The Spanish Inquisition. It is a brilliant Palin sketch with nice support from Jones and a rare – if reasonably mute – performance from Terry Gilliam, who is obviously practising for his jailer role in *The Life of Brian* ('He's … he's …. he's … m…m…m…m…MAD sir!').

At the end of the show there is more playing with the form of TV shows, as the Spanish Inquisition try to get to the Old Bailey before the end of the show. The characters – on a London bus – read the credits off the screen while commenting that they are running out of time. At the end, Palin, Jones and Gilliam burst through the door of the court and Palin starts his line only to be cut off by the arrival of a big caption saying THE END. 'Oh Bugger,' he shouts as the show draws to a close.

Series Two Show Three

Recorded as Show Five on 16 July 70
Transmitted on 29 September 70
A Bishop Rehearsing; Flying Lessons; Hijacked Plane (to Luton); The Poet McTeagle; Psychiatrist Milkman; Complaints; Déjà Vu.

Series Two Show Four

Recorded as Show Nine on 18 September 70
Transmitted on 20 October 70
Architects; How to Give up Being a Mason; Motor Insurance; The Bishop; Living Room on Pavement; Poets; A Choice of Viewing; Chemist Sketch; Words Not to be Used Again; Aftershave; Vox Pops; Police Constable PanAm.

Eric Idle gets all Napoleonic.

This show boasts not only the Architects sketch, which has Cleese's brilliant speech about Freemasons ('You wouldn't let me in, would you, you black-balling bastards') but also the fully formed Gumby (several of them actually) wandering around as a group introducing the sketches. And even more 'postmodern deconstruction' is going on within the sketches themselves, as characters ask if they have any more lines to read, while others check in the script to see if they can leave.

Show Four also has The Bishop – a terrific pastiche of late-60s action-adventure series. But more than that, this show sports brilliant opening titles ('C of E films in association with the Sunday Schools Board present: the Bishop') shot in film in black and white. Here the *Pythons* demonstrate the attention to detail we see later in the feature films. These titles are so good they use them three times. And why not?

Remember the Chemist sketch in this show? The main part of it has a long list of fish-flavoured aftershaves (essentially a long list of types of fish) – with each particular aftershave not being available. This was based on an old Chapman–Cleese sketch from pre-*Python* days, where, instead of aftershave, it was cheese. Later, for their live concerts, the sketch was converted back to the cheese format.

Series Two Show Five

Recorded as Show Seven on 10 September 70

Transmitted on 27 October 70

Live From the Grill-O-Mat Snack Bar, Paignton; Blackmail; Society for Putting Things on Top of Other Things; Escape (from film); Current Affairs; Accidents; Seven Brides for Seven Brothers; The Man Who Is Alternately Rude and Polite; Documentary on Boxer.

Series Two Show Six

Recorded as Show Eight on 10 September 70

Transmitted on 3 November 70

It's a Living; The Time on BBC1; School Prizegiving; If: A Film by Mr Dibley; Rear Window: A Film by Mr Dibley; Finian's Rainbow (starring the man from the off-licence); Foreign Secretary; Dung; Dead Indian; Timmy Williams Interview; Raymond Luxury Yacht Interview; Registry Office; Election Night Special (Silly and Sensible Parties).

More side-splitting ribaldry between takes on Monty Python's Flying Circus.

Show Six sees the opening titles relegated to the third item, after two sketches. Then Cleese's announcer appears and, instead of saying 'And now for something completely different', rather bizarrely apologises for not being able to appear. This one also has the Timmy Williams Interview, in which a chap who has just recently been widowed goes to his friend (a TV star) for money and support – which the TV star is far too self-obsessed to give.

Towards the end of this show is a Gilliam animation called The Spot – about a cancer spot that falls in love with another cancer spot and settles down and has a family. In the original programme the voiceover referred to it as a cancer, but in the repeats and videos it is – badly – overdubbed with the word 'gangrene'. Apparently this is because gangrene is funny, and cancer isn't.

The end of the show is an Election Night Special introducing us to the Sensible Party and the Silly Party – which can be directly linked to the Monster Raving Loony Party of today. Ian Davison (a regular in both Series One and Two) is the character who says to camera that this is the first time he has been on television. He also says this will probably be the last time he will be on TV (not true, as he appears in the next show).

The character of Timmy Williams is almost certainly based on David Frost, for whom most of the team had written and performed (members of the *Python* team have since been reported explaining that it was loosely based on Frost). This is unusual for the *Python*s because their material was always idea based and not – until now – referencing a real person. It is also noteworthy for its sharpness: the Timmy Williams character is really rather nasty, and, although character assassination wasn't something the *Python*s did very often, it says a lot about what they thought of Frost.

Series Two Show Seven

Recorded as Show Eleven on 2 October 70
Transmitted on 10 November 70
The Attila the Hun Show; Attila the Nun; Secretary of State Striptease; Vox Pops on Politicians; Ratcatcher; Wainscoting; Killer Sheep; The News for Parrots; The News for Gibbons; Today in Parliament; The News for Wombats; Attila the Bun; The Idiot in Society; Test Match; The Epsom Furniture Race; Take Your Pick.

Attila the Nun/Bun and Hun.

Series Two Show Eight

Recorded as Show Twelve on 9 October 70

Transmitted on 17 November 70

Trailer: Archaeology Today; Silly Vicar; Leapy Lee; Registrar (wife swap); Silly Doctor (immediately abandoned); Mr and Mrs Git; Mosquito Hunters; Poofy Judges; Mrs Thing and Mrs Entity; Beethoven's Mynah Bird; Shakespeare; Michaelangelo; Colin Mozart (ratcatcher); Judges.

Show Eight marks a sea change for *Python*: a lot of small ideas we have seen in other shows are done large here. It starts with the BBC globe and a continuity announcement; sketches are started and then immediately abandoned. We even get an animated reference to a previous sketch as a giant hedgehog appears (Spiny Norman) looking for Dinsdale (a reference to the Piranha Brothers sketch in the first show of this series).

The show ends with the two camp judges, as Eric Idle and Michael Palin reprise (in a rather more camped-up way) their characters from the Hermit sketch in Series One.

Poofy judges live at the Hollywood Bowl.

By now the audience is in on the joke and is having a whale of a time – this show would have been recorded after the series had started being broadcast. But, alas, the overall effect for the viewer isn't as good and the show has a disjointed feel. This show was recorded as Show Twelve (just one more to go in the series) and it is apparent that the ideas are running thin. In the next show (broadcast as Show Nine but recorded as Show Ten), Cleese reflects this sentiment: after a character points out that a line was particularly weak, he says, 'Well, it is the end of the series.'

Series Two Show Nine

Recorded as Show Ten on 25 September 70

Transmitted on 24 November 70

How to Recognise Different Parts of the Body; Bruces; Naughty Bits; The Man Who Contradicts People; Cosmetic Surgery; Camp Square-Bashing; Cut-Price Airline; Batley Townswomen's Guild Presents the First Heart Transplant; The First Underwater Production of Measure for Measure; The Death of Mary Queen of Scots; Exploding Penguin on TV Set; There's Been a Murder; Europolice Song Contest: 'Bing Tiddle Tiddle Bong' (song).

Show Nine has dropped the 'It's Man'. It does have the standout Bruce sketch ('Nahhww Poofters') which has irritated Australians ever since. This was the second (and last) Eric Idle and John Cleese sketch *Python* ever used. The show also has the 'Men of the Second Armoured Division doing their close-order swanning about'.

It is becoming apparent that more and more of the *Python* sketches are about homosexuals and camp behaviour, but there seems not to be any point to them other than simply laughing at campness (around this time the show's critics were preparing the phrase 'schoolboy humour' to describe it).

Gilliam seems to be getting more animations in the shows, making them even more surreal. In this one we have the Killer Cars (introduced by the sublime animation of a little old lady tripping up a double-decker bus).

Series Two Show Ten

Recorded as Show Two on 2 July 70

Transmitted on 1 December 70

French Subtitled Film; Scott of the Antarctic; Scott of the Sahara; Fish Licence; Derby Council V All Blacks Rugby Match; Long John Silver Impersonators V Bournemouth Gynaecologists.

Show Ten (which had been recorded second) doesn't run the opening titles for seventeen minutes. The beginning was done almost entirely on film (the *Python*s had been given more time and money to increase the location content in this series). It soon moves into a pastiche of the American adventure movie *Scott of the Antarctic* (which for complicated reasons is changed to Scott of the Sahara). The role of the film's mad Scottish director, who wanders around getting drunk saying 'Great ... great ...

Series two

'I would like to buy a fish licence, please!'

shoot it ...', is played to the full by John Cleese. Later the *Pythons* owned up: it was based on Ian MacNaughton – the producer-director of *Monty Python* – who was a Scot, enjoyed a drink, and was prone to saying 'great' a lot.

This show has perhaps the best of all Gilliam's animations, Conrad Pooh's Amazing Dancing Teeth. Cleese also gets to reprise his plastic-mac-wearing, greased-down-hair character we first met in the Parrot sketch, although this time he's looking for a fish licence for his pet fish Eric.

Series Two Show Eleven

Recorded as Show Six on 23 July 70
Transmitted on 8 December 70
Conquistador Coffee Campaign; Repeating Groove; Ramsay Macdonald Striptease; Job Hunter; Agatha Christie (railway timetable); Mr Neville Shunte; Film Director (teeth); City Gents Vox Pops; Crackpot Religions Ltd; How Not to Be Seen; Crossing the Atlantic on a Tricycle; Interview in Filing Cabinet; Yummy Yummy; *Monty Python's Flying Circus* Again in Thirty Seconds.

Series Two Show Twelve

Recorded as Show One on 25 June 70
Transmitted on 15 December 70
The Black Eagle; Dirty Hungarian Phrasebook; Court (phrasebook); Communist Quiz; Ypres 1914: Abandoned; Art Gallery Strike; Ypres 1914; Hospital for Overactors; Gumby Flower Arranging; Spam.

The sketch that was an instant classic from this show is the Spam sketch, despite there being a vaguely stunned air from the studio audience during recording. Written by Terry Jones and Michael Palin, it nearly didn't get into the show as both John Cleese and Graham Chapman didn't like it. But, as Eric Idle and Terry Gilliam did, the sketch stayed. Thanks, boys.

Show Twelve looks more like a Series One show, with its neatly dovetailed jokes and glimpses of behind-the-scenes mayhem. This is probably explained by the fact that it was recorded on 25 June 1970 and was actually the first show of the second series – and was eventually broadcast as the twelfth in the series, on 15 December 1970. The reasons as to why it was delayed so long in transmission are lost to history, but it serves to highlight how *Monty Python's Flying Circus* changes shape over a relatively short run of thirteen.

Series Two Show Thirteen

Recorded as Show Thirteen on 16 October 70

Transmitted on 22 December 70

The Queen Will Be Watching; Coal Mine (historical argument); The Man Who Says Things in a Very Roundabout Way; The Man Who Speaks Only the Ends of Words; The Man Who Speaks Only the Beginnings of Words; The Man Who Speaks Only the Middles of Words; Commercials; How to Feed a Gold Fish; The Man Who Collects Birdwatchers' Eggs; Insurance; Hospital Run by RSM; Mountaineer; Exploding Version of the Blue Danube; Girls' Boarding School; Submarine; Lifeboat (cannibalism); The Undertaker.

A Gumby flower arranging – live.

The last of the series to be both recorded and broadcast starts with a grave announcement from Cleese (as a BBC announcer) that the Queen may well be watching the show during the transmission. The culmination of The Queen Will Be Watching sketch marks the next phase for *Python*. When they hear the news that she is indeed watching the show, Cleese and Idle, who are in the middle of a sketch, stand up. Then we hear that the Queen has switched channels to watch *News at Ten* and we ourselves go to *News at Ten* with the then presenter Reginald Bosanquet. As he reads the news the national anthem starts and he stands up, continuing with the news, while we go back to another *Python* sketch on the BBC.

This is the clout that *Monty Python* now had within the world of television: to get the *News at Ten* team to let them shoot at their studios, with their presenter, was no mean feat. It also shows how the show was developing – using an ITV show and presenter on the BBC raised a few eyebrows and paved the way for even more 'playing with the form' later on.

But as the last in the series it wasn't going to go quietly, and the last sketch of the series – The Undertaker sketch – made sure of that. It was another John Cleese and Graham Chapman creation, this time Cleese playing a man who is trying to organise the burial of his mother. During the discussion it is suggested that the undertaker (Chapman) and Cleese eat her. This causes uproar in the studio and the audience start to catcall and boo the sketch. Before too long there is an invasion of the set by the audience – led by *Python* stalwart Ian Davison.

The whole thing was staged. The BBC would allow the sketch to be broadcast only if the *Python*s demonstrated that it was 'clearly in poor taste and not to the approval of the studio audience'. Despite getting it through with a contrived studio revolt, the next day saw the media having a field day, complaining loudly about a lack of taste from the BBC. This sketch is edited out from some of the tapes of this show.

Python had well and truly arrived in the public consciousness.

Series Three

Series Three came just over a year later, shot between December 1971 and May 1972, but by now it seemed that the BBC were a bit wiser to the ways of the *Python*. The series wasn't transmitted until the following October – five months after the last show had been taped – suggesting that the corporation was giving itself plenty of time to vet the new shows.

Series Three Show One – 'Wicker's World'

Recorded as Show Five on 14 January 72
Transmitted on 19 October 72
Court Scene: Multiple Murderer; Icelandic Saga; Court Scene (Viking); Stock Exchange Report; Mrs Premise and Mrs Conclusion Visit Jean Paul Sartre; Wicker's Island.

An island of Wickers.

In keeping with the *Python* tradition, Show One was actually the fifth recorded. As would be expected, it had new opening titles. They were a much quicker way into the show: Cleese's 'And now for something completely different' line is cut to 'And now ...', and there is just a quick shot of the 'It's Man' saying 'it's'. Then there are the Gilliam opening titles, with the show getting started right away, but not before we see Terry Jones naked playing the electric organ – a sight we get quite accustomed to in this series.

The show ends with a spoof of Alan Wicker set on Wicker Island ('There are too many Wickers on Wicker Island') where everyone is, funnily enough, Alan Wicker. The sketch is reported to have irritated the man, but more importantly it's the start of *Python* directly impersonating people.

Also, instead of sketches dovetailing into each other, they now tend to start back to back – one sketch ends and the camera moves over to the next one starting on another set.

Series Three Show Two

Recorded as Show Seven on 28 January 72
Transmitted on 26 October 72
Emigration from Surbiton to Hounslow;
Schoolboys Life Assurance Company; How to Rid
the World of All Known Diseases; Mr Niggerbaiter
Explodes; Vicar/Salesman; Farming Club; Life of
Tchaikovsky'; Trim-Jeans Theatre; Fish-Slapping Dance; The
First World War; The BBC Is Short of Money; Puss in Boots.

Series Three Show Three

Recorded as Show One on 4 December 71
Transmitted on 2 November 72
The Money Programme; There Is Nothing Quite as Wonderful as Money
(song); Elizabeth L; Fraud Film; Squad; Salvation Fuzz; Jungle
Restaurant; Apology for Violence and Nudity; Ken Russell's Gardening
Club; The Lost World of Roiurama; Six More Minutes of *Monty Python's
Flying Circus*; Argument Clinic; Hitting on the Head Lessons; Inspector
Flying Fox of the Yard; One More Minute Of *Monty Python's Flying
Circus*.

Palin gets ready for some fish-slapping.

By now, the sketches seem less and less focussed. Chapman's army character has none of the energy of the early shows and, more importantly, isn't used to move the show on. Lots of sketches refer to the fact that they are sketches and the players discuss how funny or not they are. Whereas, previously, cutting away to the BBC logo was part of a conspiracy to surprise the viewer, now the cut to the logo is done (as the announcer admits) 'Just to annoy you'.

Show Three surpasses itself in the sending-the-viewer-the-wrong-way stakes. It starts off in a chat-show studio, with Lulu and Ringo Starr, where we see the 'It's Man' arrive. But the instant he starts to announce what the show is about (he gets as far as 'it's …', so no big surprises there) the *Python* theme starts up and both stars walk out in a huff. Immediately after the *Python* opening titles, we see the opening titles of the BBC's *Money Programme*, and if you aren't careful you think you're watching the wrong show. Until, that is, we see Eric Idle as the show's presenter. He gets up and sings a song – another feature of this series being more musical numbers. But it's the trend of using famous people in the show that reflects the *Circus*'s popularity with not only the general public but with showbiz too.

The show ends and we see the BBC globe logo. Then the announcer tells us that there are still six minutes left and we are thrown back to the show. The last sketch is the famous Argument sketch ('Is this a five-minute argument or the full half-hour?'), proving that the team is still capable of producing classic material.

Series Three Show Four

Recorded as Show Two on 11 December 71

Transmitted on 9 November 72

Blood, Devastation, Death, War and Horror; The Man Who Speaks in Anagrams; Anagrams Quiz; Merchant Banker; Pantomime Horses; Life and Death Struggles; Mary Recruitment Office; The Bus Conductor; The Man Who Makes People Laugh Uncontrollably; Army Captain as Clown; Gestures to Indicate Pauses in a Televised Talk; Neurotic Announcers; The News With Richard Baker (vision only); The Pantomime Horse Is a Secret Agent Film.

There are still flashes of brilliance in the new style. In the last series the *Python*s roped in the ITV news; in this show we have Richard Baker – a senior BBC newsreader – reading the news. Although we don't hear him, he acts out some of the gestures used in the previous sketch. Again this reminds us of the status *Python*s had achieved at the BBC. Anagrams are the theme here, and the closing credits call the show *Tony M Nyphot's Flying Risccu*.

Favourite Python *characters reprised during the shooting of* The Life of Brian.

Series Three Show Five - 'The All England Summarise Proust Competition'

Recorded as Show Nine on 24 April 72

Transmitted on 16 November 72

Summarise Proust Competition; Everest Climbed by Hairdressers; Fire Brigade; Our Eamonn; Party Hints With Veronica Smalls; Language Laboratory; Travel Agent; Watney's Red Barrel; Theory on Brontosaurus by Anne Elk (Miss).

Show Five has the holiday sketch, a long speech about people on holiday in Spain with lots of references to Watney's Red Barrel (a beer). This was a Cleese and Chapman sketch, but no one wanted to do it because of the extended speech at the end. Everyone except Eric Idle, that is, who would go on to recite this rambling monologue every time *Python* played a stage show for years to come (and you can't blame him really. Having gone to all the bother of memorising it, it would seem a bit churlish to use it only the once).

We also get a classic Cleese–Chapman creation, The Summarising Proust Competition, which just went to highlight that, no matter how silly the *Python*s could get, they still had their intellectual roots in the scholarly pursuits of Oxbridge.

Series Three Show Six

Recorded as Show Six on 21 January 72
Transmitted on 23 November 72
Tory Housewives' Clean-Up Campaign; Gumby Brain Specialist; Molluscs: Live TV Documentary; The Minister for Not Listening to People; Tuesday Documentary/Children's Story/Party Political Broadcast; Apology (politicians); Expedition to Lake Pahoe; The Silliest Interview We've Ever Had; The Silliest Sketch We've Ever Done.

Series Three Show Seven

Recorded as Show Four on 7 January 72
Transmitted on 30 November 72
Biggles Dictates a Letter; Climbing the North Face of the Uxbridge Road; Lifeboat; Old Lady Snoopers; Storage Jars; The Show So Far; Cheese Shop; Philip Jenkinson on Cheese Westerns; Sam Peckinpah's Salad Days; Apology; The News With Richard Baker; Seashore Interlude Film.

Show Seven gave us a couple of items still remembered today. 'My brain hurts' from the Gumbys is a favourite, but less well remembered is the Sam Peckinpah pastiche called Salad Days – a much underrated parody. Sam Peckinpah was the Tarantino of his day, and his films were renowned for being very violent and bloody. In the hands of the *Python*s, we're watching a film of a 1920s picnic – all boaters and stripped blazers – where Palin serves at tennis only to watch the racket slip from his hands and disembowel Carol Cleveland. It then gets very messy as numerous arms and legs are accidentally pulled off.

The BBC received many complaints for this sketch, but it was further evidence of how well the team was working with film. While the sketch was simply that, a sketch, its execution and attention to detail was a harbinger of what was to come on the big screen. All the same, this show is overshadowed by another in the pantheon of *Python* classics: the Cheese Shop. Using the format that they had developed earlier, Cleese and Chapman do that thing with the list of cheeses. It's a classic ('But I'm afraid the Camembert's a bit runny, sir').

Series Three Show Eight – 'The Cycling Tour'

Recorded as Show Ten on 4 May 72
Transmitted on 7 December 72
Mr Pither; Clodagh Rogers; Trotsky; Smolensk; Bingo-Crazed Chinese; Jack in a Box.

Show **Eight**, 'The Cycling Tour', is generally seen to be the weakest of the series. Recorded as Show Ten, it is a rehash of an earlier – rejected – attempt at a Ripping Yarns script by Terry Jones and Michael Palin, but with the rest of the team pulling in different directions it has the feeling of being an overstretched sketch thin on ideas.

Series Three Show Nine

Recorded as Show Eleven on 25 May 72
Transmitted on 14 December 72
Bomb on Plane; A Naked Man; Ten Seconds of Sex; Housing Project Built by Characters From Nineteenth-Century English Literature; M1 Interchange Built by Characters From Paradise Lost; Mystico and Janet: Flats Built by Hypnosis; Mortuary Hour; The Olympic Hide and Seek Final; The Cheap Laughs; Bull Fighting; The British Well-Basically Club; Prices on the Planet Algon.

There is a growing feeling that the series is devouring itself as it looks for more and more things to deconstruct, and the introduction to Show Nine is a prime example. The first thing we see is nude organ man (Terry Jones) giving what sounds like a highbrow interview, but he cuts his conversation short to do his bit. We then cut to Cleese as the BBC announcer discussing the basics of comedy

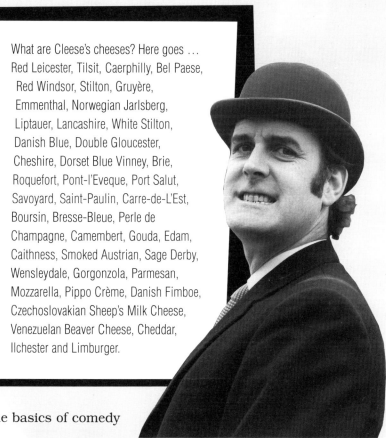

What are Cleese's cheeses? Here goes … Red Leicester, Tilsit, Caerphilly, Bel Paese, Red Windsor, Stilton, Gruyère, Emmenthal, Norwegian Jarlsberg, Liptauer, Lancashire, White Stilton, Danish Blue, Double Gloucester, Cheshire, Dorset Blue Vinney, Brie, Roquefort, Pont-l'Eveque, Port Salut, Savoyard, Saint-Paulin, Carre-de-L'Est, Boursin, Bresse-Bleue, Perle de Champagne, Camembert, Gouda, Edam, Caithness, Smoked Austrian, Sage Derby, Wensleydale, Gorgonzola, Parmesan, Mozzarella, Pippo Crème, Danish Fimboe, Czechoslovakian Sheep's Milk Cheese, Venezuelan Beaver Cheese, Cheddar, Ilchester and Limburger.

An off-licence sketch.

with someone until he realises he is on camera, and says, 'And now ...' Finally we get to the 'It's Man' saying 'it's' (with no extra dialogue) and the show starts. But this protracted beginning doesn't stop here. Even Gilliam gets in on the act, and as we go to an animation we catch him explaining how they're done. When he realises we've seen this, he appears as himself (in animation form) to apologise. At the end of the show you're left with the feeling that there isn't much more to deconstruct. Except the deconstructions.

Series Three Show Ten

Recorded as Show Thirteen on 25 May 72

Transmitted on 21 December 72

Tudor Job Agency; Pornographic Bookshop; Elizabethan Pornography Smugglers; Silly Disturbances (the Rev. Arthur Belling); The Free Repetition of Doubtful Words, by an Underrated Author; Is There? ... Life After Death?; The Man Who Says Words in the Wrong Order; Thripshaw's Disease; Silly Noises; Sherry-Drinking Vicar.

Series Three Show Eleven

Recorded as Show Eight on 17 April 72

Transmitted on 4 January 73

Boxing Tonight: Jack Bodell V Sir Kenneth Clark; Dennis Moore; Lupins; What the Stars Foretell; Doctor; TV4 or Not TV4 Discussion; Ideal Loon Exhibition; Off-Licence; Prejudice.

Series Three Show Twelve

Recorded as Show Three on 18 December 71

Transmitted on 11 January 73

Party Political Broadcast (choreographed); A Book at Bedtime; Redgauntlet Kamikaze Scotsmen; No Time to Lose; Penguins; BBC Programme Planners; Unexploded Scotsman; Spot the Loony; Rival Documentaries; Dad's Doctors (trail); Dad's Pooves (trail).

Series Three Show Thirteen – 'Grandstand'

Recorded as Show Twelve on 18 May 72

Transmitted on 18 January 73

Thames TV Introduction; Light Entertainment Awards; Dickie Attenborough; Oscar Wilde; David Niven's Fridge; Pasolini's Film: The Third Test Match; New Brains From Curry's; Blood Donor; International Wife Swapping; Credits of the Year; The Dirty Vicar Sketch.

The series ends with a, by now, typical *Python* start. David Hamilton – then a continuity announcer for Thames TV, an ITV station – opens the show. He is sitting in his studio saying, 'We have an action-packed evening tonight on Thames, but right now a rotten old BBC programme.' We are now in no doubt that it is the medium that's now the fodder for *Monty Python*, although the show represents some return to form in the shape of the Oscar Wilde sketch ('You will, Oscar, you will'). But you just can't get away from the feeling that this is the team filling time – the linking is tired and the sketches overlong.

A gratuitous Wicker shot.

Series Four

Cleese had not been happy with *Monty Python* during Series Three and felt that the show had run its course – and maybe in retrospect he was right.

In October 1974, when the fourth and last series came to be made, Cleese was loudly absent, having told his fellow *Python*s, on a tour to Canada, that he would no longer be taking part. The others – also with their own projects bubbling under the surface – toyed with the idea of packing it in themselves, but they decided to give it a go without Cleese.

The shows still had Ian MacNaughton at the production helm, and Idle's chum Neil Innes and *Hitchhiker's Guide to the Galaxy* writer Douglas Adams were given opportunities to write for the show. Perhaps to acknowledge the fact that this wasn't the show that had started back in 1969, the series title was reduced to *Monty Python*. Cleese had taken the Flying Circus with him. But this wasn't the only change.

Interestingly, the shows were put out in recording order (a first for *Python*) and only a matter of weeks after they had been

Chapman gets bullied by Palin's selfish policeman.

shot. Obviously the BBC had a wholly different view of the show by now, and were even prepared to boast about it. It may have been a mutual backing down on all sides, because in this series there was only one real sideswipe at the BBC, in the Programme Planners sketch. In retrospect it seems that the BBC knew, somehow, that the shows were not going to be as dangerous as before, or were at least prepared to take the hit if the *Pythons* crossed the line into bad taste. But then, in the context of a new libertarianism in broadcasting, the *Pythons* simply weren't as shocking as they had been years previously. The world had caught up with them.

Series Four Show One – 'The Golden Age of Ballooning'

Recorded as Show One on 12 October 74

Transmitted on 31 October 74

The Montgolfier Brothers; Louis XIV; George III; Zeppelin.

Much of the material for this series came from ideas Jones and Palin had prepared – but not used – for the project that eventually gave us *Monty Python and the Holy Grail*. And from the very first show it was painfully obvious that this wasn't the *Python* of old. It had all the hallmarks of *Python*: a false start ('The Golden Age of Ballooning'), and then not running the opening credits until the very end of the show (and then promptly running the closing credits directly after). But the content of the shows is really only of interest to die-hard fans. The series was on its last legs and, despite some spirited ideas, is more of historical interest than something likely to make you laugh.

Much like the Bicycling Holiday in the previous series, this show had just one theme – ballooning. A lot of the same characters lasted throughout the show, but the sketches seem to go nowhere. Cleese is credited on the writing front – his material was still being used for most of the series – but his (often irritating and pedantic) approach to script editing and quality control is sorely missed here.

Series Four Show Two – 'Michael Ellis'

Recorded as Show Two on 19 October 74

Transmitted on 7 November 74

Department Store; Buying an Ant; At Home With the Ant and Other Pets; Documentary on Ants; Ant Communication; Poetry Reading (ants); Toupee; Different Endings.

Show Two takes the idea of playing with the credits to the [n]th degree by running the end credits directly after the opening titles. This is the Michael Ellis show where Eric Idle is confused with a chap called Michael Ellis, an idea milked to the very end. There is a Buying an Ant sketch which has all the hallmarks of a Graham Chapman and John Cleese script, but mostly the show moves along at half-speed.

Interestingly, Gilliam gets one of the largest roles in a sketch in all four series. With one performer down, the *Python*s get Gilliam in front of the camera more than ever before.

As if to underscore the lack of direction of the whole fourth series, this show ends with a discussion between Jones and Idle about how the programme should end. What does Idle want: a happy ending, a sad ending, a fade out or what? After a couple of suggestions, Jones says how about a sudden ending – and that's what happens; it all goes black.

Series Four Show Three – 'Light Entertainment War'

Recorded as Show Three on 26 October 74

Transmitted on 14 November 74

Up Your Pavement; RAF Banter; Trivialising the War; Court Martial; Basingstoke in Westphalia; Anything Goes In (song); Film Trailer; The Public Are Idiots; Programme Titles Conference; The Last Five Miles of the M2; Woody and Tinny Words; Show Jumping (musical); News Flash (Germans); When Does a Dream Begin? (song).

Show Three sees a return to a more traditional *Python* structure, with sketches that stand on their own. This is the first time we see Neil Innes on screen. He had been working on both musical material and parts of the sketches before now, and at long last gets to sing a song. Combined with the steady stream of songs, celebrity appearances and impressions of famous people, this episode feels disturbingly like a variety show.

Series Four Show Four – 'Hamlet'

Recorded as Show Four on 2 November 74

Transmitted on 21 November 74

Bogus Psychiatrists; Nationwide; Police Helmets; Father-in-Law; Hamlet and Ophelia; Boxing Match Aftermath; Boxing Commentary; Piston Engine (a bargain); A Room in Polonius's House; Dentists; Live From Epsom; Queen Victoria Handicap.

Series Four Show Five – 'Mr Nutron'

Recorded as Show Five on 9 November 74

Transmitted on 28 November 74

Postbox Ceremony; Teddy Salad (CIA agent); Conjuring Today.

Series Four Show Six – 'Party Political Broadcast'

Recorded as Show Six on 16 November 74

Transmitted on 5 December 74

Most Awful Family in Britain; Icelandic Honey Week; A Doctor Whose Patients Are Stabbed by His Nurse; Brigadier and Bishop; Appeal on Behalf of Extremely Rich People; The Man Who Finishes Other People's Sentences; David Attenborough; The Walking Tree of Dahomey; The Batsman of the Kalahari; Cricket Match (assegais); BBC News (handovers).

 I ronically, *the last* ever *Monty Python* television show breaks new ground. It is the first that credits writers beyond the *Python* crew, with both Neil Innes and Douglas Adams getting a mention on the credits. The Most Awful Family in Britain is probably the best sketch of the series, but it's still a long way from the glory days of Series One and Two.

There was an interesting role reversal with this series: the BBC, suddenly waking up to the fact that the mould of British comedy had been changed by *Python* (and that the public liked it), wanted to put out more shows. As volte-faces go, this was sublime – the BBC, having spent years trying to hide the show in the schedules under dusty piles of programming, forcing editorial changes on it and generally attempting to disown it, now wanted more.

Michael Palin thought this was a good idea and lobbied the group to do another six; but Eric Idle had had enough. When Idle vetoed the idea of more shows; an era in television history closed. *Monty Python's Flying Circus* was dead. It was no more. Bereft of life, it rests in peace.

But then, out of the ashes, rose a new *Monty Python*. The *Monty Python* of the movies. And that was something completely different.

This series is notable for the number of different faces on screen, lots of extras (almost certainly a result of bigger budgets) and Carol Cleveland being given proper roles to play. Cleese is still getting a writing credit and his then wife Connie Booth almost matches Cleveland in screen time.

Palin's BBC newsreader.

Monty Python
Goes to the Movies

That the Pythons should choose to go into film is probably the single most important decision they ever made. Their first not-too-successful attempt at the movies was a collection of sketches called *And Now for Something Completely Different*, but it was a rehash of television material put together for the big screen and didn't extend their unique skills any more than the TV shows. And, as the last series of the television shows had demonstrated, the TV format was stale. The *Pythons* needed a new creative outlet to continue.

With *Monty Python and the Holy Grail* this was exactly what they got. It put them firmly on the map once more, and rejuvenated their sense of doing something different and slightly dangerous. Its success also meant that Cleese, who had seen himself very much as a peripheral *Python* up until then, was back in the club with a vengeance.

Their next film, *The Life of Brian*, is probably regarded as their *tour de force*, and rightly so. Its rip-roaring, continual narrative once again stretched the boundaries of what *Python* represented, and set them firmly on an international stage as world-class film-makers.

Their third and last film, *The Meaning of Life*, took them back to their roots with a series of sketches all connected under a single theme. It was met with a mixed critical reaction, but was, without a doubt, the most shocking piece of cinema they'd ever done.

Love them or loathe them, the *Pythons* had turned cinema on its head, and together the four films represent a staggering achievement, a canon of work that has immortalised their disparate talents for generations of fans to come. There's no getting away from it. These are *funny, funny* people.

And Now for Something Completely Different

Released September 1971 – 88 minutes

After the success of the first two TV series, the *Monty Python* bandwagon started to gather momentum, and one of the people it ran over in 1970 was London Playboy Club entrepreneur Victor Lownes. Lownes was a big fan of the show and had astutely realised the potential for its unique brand of humour in America, where he figured a movie of the best sketches from the TV series would be a perfect introduction for US viewers (particularly students). Lownes convinced the *Python*s that it would be an opportunity for them to make large sums of money as well as giving them an invaluable foothold in the American market. He was proved wrong on both counts.

With a budget of £80,000, the group asked Ian MacNaughton – who was in charge of the TV shows – to direct the film. He agreed, and together they cherry-picked the best sketches for the move to the big screen. Practically identical to their TV originals but glued together with some fresh linking material, the sketches were filmed over five weeks in October and November 1970 at a disused milk depot in north London and in Totteridge.

Trouble started brewing early on when Lownes – no doubt thinking that it was his money and he could spend it exactly how he wanted – began to interfere with the content and style of the film. Unfortunately for Lownes, the *Python*s had enjoyed a free rein at the BBC, where producer Barry Took had wisely stepped back from the artistic process and allowed them to create 'from the ground upwards'. Not surprisingly, having a rather pushy financier breathing down their necks and making suggestions for the sketches proved unpopular with all of the *Python*s. In one of their many battles, Lownes successfully banned Michael Palin's character Ken Shabby from the film on the basis that he was too grotesque. And so, despite the character's popularity in the TV shows, Shabby failed to make an appearance in the film. Further acrimony broke out when Gilliam initially refused Lownes's request to incorporate his name in the opening credits in the grandiose style of *Ben Hur*.

All these issues would have been irrelevant, of course, had the film succeeded – or at least met its expectations of success. But alas it made little money in the UK and sank like a stone in the US, despite favourable reviews on both sides of the Atlantic. To make matters worse, the launch of the film in America was marred by distribution and publicity problems, which stole the thunder of *Python*'s arrival. In retrospect, Lownes was right about the potential for the *Python*s in the US, because four years later their TV shows began broadcasting on public-service television and an instant cult following

Idle's marriage guidance counsellor makes the move to the big screen.

was established. Unfortunately for Lownes and the *Pythons* alike, *And Now for Something Completely Different* was ahead of its time.

Critical opinion is divided on the merits of the film. Some say the higher production values make the sketches more accessible than the TV shows and that the film successfully captures early *Python* for subsequent generations. Others say the performances in the film have little to offer above the television shows and that a cobbled together 'best of' film was a shabby compromise for a comedy group that was being truly radical.

Whichever opinion holds sway, *And Now for Something Completely Different* gave the *Pythons* an invaluable insight into how the production of a movie differed from the making of a TV series. For Gilliam and Jones particularly it gave the confidence to go on to further film projects, experience that would pay dividends when the *Pythons* made their second film, *Monty Python and the Holy Grail*, in 1975.

The film is also notable for one small fact – it's the only *Python* film to feature a *Blue Peter* presenter, in this case a young Leslie Judd in a walk-on part.

It's

Michael Palin crawls out of the sea, Robinson Crusoe-like, and staggers to camera to utter the ever present one-word beginning to every *Monty Python* show. 'It's ...' he intones, before the rousing *Monty Python* theme music heralds a typically creative animation from Terry Gilliam.

How Not to be Seen

Narrated by John Cleese, some wonderfully named suburbanites such as Mrs BJ Smegma are blown to smithereens using far better special effects than were ever seen in the TV series. Cleese's no-nonsense public-information voice not only shows us how not to be seen, but generously explains why it's important not to be seen.

Man in the Dinner Jacket

Cleese again, as the TV announcer seated behind a desk, linking items using the film's title. Throughout the film this announcer appears in ever more illogical and unfeasible situations.

Animated Titles

Terry Gilliam's trademark animations both begin and, very abruptly, end the film.

Theatre Compere

Michael Palin, looking very shady in an ill-fitting suit and with his hair slicked back, furtively smokes a cigarette as he slips out from behind the cinema curtain to apologise for the premature end of the film. In desperation, he announces the next act – A Man With a Tape Recorder up His Nose.

A Man With a Tape Recorder up His Nose

A sepia-tinted Terry Jones, dressed in vaudevillian coat and tails, proudly demonstrates his tape-recorder technique by sticking a finger of his white-gloved hand up his nose. We are rewarded with a brief snatch of the French national anthem, which Terry kindly rewinds by sticking his finger up his other nostril. He is joined by Graham Chapman (making Jones A Man With a Tape Recorder up His Brother's Nose) so they can repeat the process in stereo.

Hungarian Phrasebook

Deliciously silly sketch where a Hungarian uses a phrasebook to try to buy some cigarettes. The book translates his innocent efforts into phrases such as 'I wunt to forndle yerr buttokks'. Michael Palin, the publisher of the phrasebook, is taken to court. Terry Jones doubles up as the shopkeeper and the judge.

Animations

Terry Gilliam gets a cartoon head to lather itself up in preparation for a shave, only to behead itself.

Marriage Guidance Counsellor

Arthur Putey and his wife (Michael Palin/Carol Cleveland) go to see Eric Idle's wonderfully lascivious marriage guidance counsellor. Idle proceeds to blatantly seduce Cleveland in front of Putey, asking him to leave the room as Cleveland undresses behind a screen. Putey sheepishly backs away until a Godlike voice urges him to be a real man. Putey declines, and is immediately squashed by a ten-tonne weight.

Animation

The hungry baby carriage, and Michelangelo's *David* trying to preserve his modesty.

Nudge Nudge

Terry Jones, dressed in the bowler-hatted uniform of the *Python* City gent, is sitting down in a pub for a quiet pint when Eric Idle's cravated wide-boy takes a seat next to him. Lampooning every *Carry On* double entendre ever written, Idle proceeds to try to strike up a laddish conversation about his sex life with the mortified and slightly incredulous Jones. Uncharacteristically for the *Python*s, the sketch ends with a classic, non-ironic punchline (it turns out the filthy-minded Idle is a virgin). 'Nudge nudge', like 'It's an ex-parrot', became a *Python* rallying cry for generations of fans – notably drunk students in union bars.

Self-Defence

John Cleese in vintage manic mode as the self-defence instructor teaching the rest of the *Python*s how to protect themselves from assailants armed with fruit ('Loganberries?'). Cleese's resort to a pistol at the end of the sketch found echoes in Hollywood years later when Harrison Ford shot a show-off swordsman in *Raiders of the Lost Ark*.

Silliness Colonel

Graham Chapman, splendidly authoritative as the Colonel, stops the film on the grounds that it's getting 'too silly'. After issuing a stern warning about being silly in the future, he allows the film to continue. It's a good job he does, because then we launch straight into a classic *Monty Python* set piece – Hell's Grannies.

Hell's Grannies

An archetypal role-reversal sketch where old ladies go around acting like teenage thugs, while teenage thugs (the hugely improbable Terry Jones) bemoan the fact they can't go out to the shops any more for fear of getting mugged. The sketch ends with a glimpse of rival gangs of baby snatchers (*Python*s dressed as babies stealing adults from outside shops).

'Likes photography, does she?'

Silliness Colonel and Camp Square-Bashing

The Colonel gives us another stiff warning about getting silly, before we see the excellently choreographed mincing soldiers doing a prancing army drill to phrases such as 'Oooh, I'll scratch yer eyes out'.

Animation

A young prince gets a spot, which soon kills him and then goes off to wreak more spot-based havoc in Gilliam's animated universe.

Kilimanjaro Expedition (double vision)

John Cleese plays Sir George Head, a hopelessly double-visioned incompetent who's leading a mountaineering expedition to 'both peaks of Kilimanjaro'. Eric Idle, a professional mountaineer ('A mountaineer? What's that?' asks a fascinated Cleese), is being interviewed for a place on the team. Mayhem ensues as Graham Chapman enters in full climbing gear to demolish the room as he shows off his traversing technique across the bookshelf. Superb payoff as the running joke about there being two Eric Idles comes full circle.

Man Not in the Dinner Jacket

John Cleese links the next item surrounded by young women wearing bikinis, while he himself looks rather fetching in a little pink two-piece.

Come Back to My Place

Michael Palin approaches a policeman (John Cleese) with an implausible report of a mugging. After a moment's silence, Palin invites the policeman back to his flat. Cleese looks around to see if anyone's watching. 'Oh, all right,' he says, and they both walk off camera.

Flasher

Terry Jones scares women.
That sounds like rather a good idea for a sketch.

Animations

A longer animated section showing Gilliam at his early best. First the Communist Chinese attack (a sketch whose reference to the Chinese as small and yellow would never make it on to the screens these days) is thwarted by Uncle Sam. Then adverts for Crelm Toothpaste, Shrill Oil and Twentieth Century Frog. It ends with the superbly foolish Conrad Poohs and His Dancing Teeth (Conrad is 'played' by Gilliam himself).

Musical Mice

A seedy nightclub plays host to Terry Jones's 'Ken Ewing and His Musical Mice' act, in which Ewing hits an array of mice 'which have been painstakingly trained over the past few years to squeak at a selected pitch'. With two comedy mallets and obvious gusto, Jones starts to play 'Three Blind Mice', before being dragged from the stage by an outraged audience and two equally outraged bouncers.

It's the Arts

Sir Edward Ross (Graham Chapman) is interviewed by John Cleese, who starts by truncating Chapman's name to Ted and ends up by calling him Eddie-Baby, much to Chapman's disgust. The interview is interrupted by the still-rampaging audience from the previous sketch breaking into the studio and chasing Jones.

'So, Eddie-baby – if I can call you that . . . ?

Seduced Milkmen

Scantily clad Carol Cleveland entices Palin's incredulous milkman indoors with a flash of her thighs. She seductively beckons him upstairs and into a bedroom, only to lock the door behind him. Palin finds himself in a room full of milkmen, some of whom appear to have been there for a very long time.

The Funniest Joke in the World

Michael Palin is Ernest Scribbler, 'a writer of jokes', who – having written the previous sketch – goes on to write a gag so funny that he dies laughing. Death and mayhem ensue until the military arrive and develop the joke as a secret weapon by translating it into German. One translator accidentally sees two words together and is hospitalised for a week. And the joke? 'Wenn ist das Nünstuck git und Slotermeyer? Ja! ... Beiherund das Oder die Flipperwaldt gersput!' This was over 60,000 times as powerful as Britain's great pre-war joke, 'My dog's got no nose ...'

A little-known sketch about a parrot.

Animation

Killer cars stalk the Earth until scientists create something to get rid of them – the killer cat. An animated *Venus de Milo* turns into a fish-tank ornament, leading seamlessly into a sketch about a parrot.

Parrot Sketch

An obscure skit, with Michael Palin as a man working in a pet shop and John Cleese as the recent purchaser of a less-than-lively Norwegian blue. Palin ends the sketch by bemoaning his career choice. 'I wanted to be lumberjack,' he cries, leading nicely on to …

The Lumberjack Song

Infamous Python ditty with Connie Booth as the luckless lumberjack's girlfriend and an assortment of Canadian Mounties as the choir. See if you can spot Terry Gilliam singing energetically in the front row.

Man in a Dinner Jacket on a Spit

Roasting above a fire, John Cleese informs us that now comes something completely different.

The Restaurant

Graham Chapman and Carol Cleveland inadvertently kill off all the staff in a restaurant when Chapman complains of a dirty fork. A tongue-in-cheek ending as Chapman turns to camera and remarks how lucky it was he didn't complain about the dirty knife as well.

Animation

Rodin's *The Lovers* becomes an ingenious wind instrument, with well-placed thigh holes.

Bank Robber

John Cleese executes a flawless robbery on a bank, only to be told he's actually holding up a ladies' lingerie store. 'No piles of cash in easy-to-carry bags, then?' he asks haplessly.

Office Window

Eric Idle and John Cleese share an unfeasibly small desk and watch apathetically as various co-workers plummet to their death past the window. 'Must be a board meeting,' says Cleese distractedly. A letter of

Graham Chapman keeps quiet about the dirty knife.

complaint follows, bemoaning the fact that the author has worked in an office for many years and he's not once seen anyone fall out of a wind ... aaaaggghhhhhhh.

Animation

Wonderfully *stylistic sequence* in which a grunting, groaning, grey caterpillar shuffles into bed only to emerge as a shiny, cheesy gameshow-host butterfly.

Vocational Guidance Counsellor

Michael Palin as an Arthur Putey-type character (in this case Mr Anchovy) who decides he wants to leave accountancy to become a lion tamer. John Cleese breaks the news that lions are not, in fact, small ant-eating animals with long snouts, but actually large ferocious beasts with long claws and sharp pointy teeth. Anchovy decides to go into lion taming via banking or insurance. Thanks to Idle's fairy godmother, Palin metapmorphs into Wally Wiggins, the host of gameshow *Blackmail*.

Blackmail

Palin *extorts money* from viewers with footage of their secret peccadilloes. Terry Jones is alarmingly naked as he plays the theme music on a Hammond organ. Caught on camera is Graham Chapman's Colonel visiting a suburban brothel. The Colonel links to the next sketch.

Batley Townswomen's Guild

In a gloriously muddy version of this much-loved skit, the *Python*s – dressed in the most frumpy middle-aged women's clothing they could find – beat the living daylights out of each other in a re-enactment of the Battle of Pearl Harbour.

Erotic Film

Terry Jones and Carol Cleveland start snogging in bed, and as things warm up we see phallic and suggestive footage of rockets rising, trains going into tunnels, and all manner of clichéd visual metaphors. It turns out that Jones and Cleveland are watching the footage as well.

Upper-Class Twit of the Year

Another iconic sketch as the *Python*s negotiate various tricky events, such as running in a straight line, waking up the neighbours and undoing a bra strap. Classic *Python*.

End Credits

A final animated sequence from Terry Gilliam

Cleese, the accidental lingerie robber.

Monty Python and the Holy Grail

Cinema 5/Columbia (US) and EMI (UK)
Released April 1975 – 90 minutes

Were it not for this ground-breaking film – the group's first feature film proper – the *Python* team would have gone their separate ways, leaving only the TV series and *And Now for Something Completely Different* as their combined comedic legacy. They had already decided to pursue individual projects – Cleese having been absent for the last TV series and Idle in the process of devising a format for his own show. The success of *Holy Grail* suddenly showed them how widespread their popularity had become, and, for the first time ever, made them some serious money. It gave the group some long-term (and long-awaited) belief in the tenability of the *Python* project.

Since the beginning of the third TV series, the group had flirted with the idea of writing a full-length film, and had begun to file away ideas and themes for sketches, with a view to resurrecting them if the notion ever came to anything. When plans firmed up and a first script was written, it was very much a typical *Python* construction – a 'mish-mash of half-modern-day, half-medieval' sketches, remembers Terry Jones. But it was felt the script needed to be more than a TV-show-plus, and Jones – who was in the process of writing a book on Chaucerian England – came up with the idea of making the show entirely medieval. Out went the idea of the knights buying the Grail in the Grail Hall at Harrods, and in came the commonality of theme that gave the film a cohesive storyline instead of being a collection of disjointed sketches. Some of the earlier ideas made it through to the final version, notably the modern-day historian who gets spectacularly sliced to death by the knights at the end, and the arrival of the police who arrest the knights and drive them away.

Even so, despite the continuity of the *Holy Grail* storyline, the film is easily segmented into smaller skits, and in evolutionary terms marks a halfway point between the sketch format of *And Now for Something Completely Different* and the cinematic largesse of *The Life of Brian*.

The finance for the film was set up by Michael White, who had arranged for *Cambridge Circus* and '****' to be brought to London some years earlier. He cast his net wide, and raised money from an eclectic bunch of backers, including rock bands Pink Floyd and Led Zeppelin. White's success at getting cash for the film masked the fact that it was still a remarkably low-budget affair – £229,000 is the oft-quoted figure – and so the *Python*s took a leap of faith and paid themselves virtually nothing, relying instead on much-hoped-for profits when the film was released (a wise decision given its commercial success and the fact that the film is still available on video today). Had the film not made money, the group would almost certainly never have performed together again, since Cleese – who felt he had been let down by Victor Lownes over promises of wealth from *And Now for Something Completely Different* – had tired of all things *Python*, and took considerable persuasion to join the crew for one final go at movie success.

Ironically, the budgetary constrictions led, inadvertently, to one of the most enduring images of *Holy Grail* – the knights using coconut shells to make clippity-clop noises instead of riding horses. Horses proved too expensive, and according to Palin the decision to use coconut shells was the point at which it seemed feasible to make the whole film set in the Middle Ages.

The film was co-directed by Terry Jones and Terry Gilliam, and was the first major project for both of them – itself a cause for infighting and friction during the shoot. The decision to have Jones and Gilliam direct and edit was more for artistic integrity than egotism. The group simply wanted to make sure nobody messed with their material. It was a decision both of them would rue in the months to come.

When Ian MacNaughton directed *And Now for Something Completely Different*, it was at his feet that all the disagreements and difficulties were laid. But, with *Holy Grail*, Jones and Gilliam had to take more executive responsibility, which left them feeling they were

The knights of the round table take a well-earned coffee break.

getting picked on by the rest of the group when things weren't going too well. 'Directing is a shitty job when it's not your project,' said Gilliam. 'I got fed up with the whole

The knights antagonise some Frenchmen.

The Knights Who Say Ni – one of the most celebrated scenes from *Holy Grail* – almost didn't make it into the film. It was a classic piece of Palin–Jones scriptwriting – absurd and utterly unexplained – and on the first few passes of the script the other *Python*s expressed doubts about whether it would work. We have to thank Palin and Jones's perseverance for a generation of long-haired engineering students stumbling drunk around town centres shouting 'We are the Knights Who Say … NIIII!!'

thing.' This was on top of the already existing divisions that had been papered over in order to get the project off the ground. All in all, production was not a pleasurable experience for anyone, including Palin, whose people skills made him into an unofficial 'fixer'.

For starters, Jones and Gilliam had eschewed the glossy, technicoloured image of the Middle Ages touted around by various Hollywood movies. Instead they went for ultra-realism, with all of the characters dressed in dirty, wet clothing and spending inordinate amounts of time wading through authentically muddy fields. Almost all of the shooting took place at a remote Scottish castle, in the most appalling weather, with the *Python*s having to stand around all day in string-knitted chain mail, cold uncomfortable helmets and shoes that were little more than leather bags tied around their feet. The net result gave the film an unexpectedly high-budget look and feel, because of its period authenticity and its dark, claustrophobic atmosphere – not much consolation to the *Python*s, who had been reduced to driving around in the back of a pick-up between shoots.

Things weren't improved by Graham Chapman's drinking, which had become dangerously intrusive to both the film and Chapman's wellbeing (he was on his way to consuming two pub-sized bottles of gin a day – eighty fluid ounces – and battling the advanced stages of alcoholism). He had valiantly decided that on the first day of the shoot he would stop drinking, a decision he stuck to for about three hours. Dressed as King Arthur, preparing for the scene where he crosses the Bridge of Death, Chapman suddenly realised that his resolve to quit might have been a tad impetuous. He started to get the delirium tremens and was horrified to discover none of the crew had any alcohol on them. Costumer Hazel Pethig recalls she couldn't get his gloves off because his hands were shaking so much. This episode – more than any other – helped Chapman steel himself for a full-scale evacuation of the Good Ship Alcoholism, which he painfully (and successfully) abandoned in December 1977.

The splendidly absurd three-headed knight.

Ironically, it was Chapman's predilection for booze that rescued the film from a premature end some ten days into the shoot. Conditions had got so bad the cast and crew were on the verge of walking out. The two Terries were pushing everyone hard, no doubt trying to prove to themselves as much as to everyone else that they had the stamina and strength of character to see the job through. But, a week and a half in, no one had yet seen any rushes (rushes are the raw footage taken on a film set and shown on a daily basis so everyone can see how the film is progressing) and morale was at an all-time low. After a day's filming that had almost culminated in a full-scale mutiny, Chapman gathered the entire cast and crew in the bar of the hotel where they

The ancient Arthurian custom of six-a-side football.

were staying and proceeded to buy drinks for the whole lot. He also kick-started an almighty singalong, an altruistic and uncharacteristic gesture from a man who was renowned for being painfully shy. It was just what the crew needed to bring about a sense of camaraderie and shared adventure. And, when the rushes were delivered the next day, the crisis had been averted.

The film's tight budget also meant that some of the scenes designed to look desperately dangerous were – in actuality – desperately dangerous. Cleese seemed to bear the brunt of most of these, swinging across tables laden with pointy props in the scene where Sir Lancelot disbands a wedding party by slaughtering the guests, and – as Tim the Enchanter – standing high on a mountain peak while explosions and high winds did their best to blow him off. Cleese drew the line at one stunt where he was supposed to run across the presciently titled Bridge of Death wearing water-logged string chain-mail and shoes with slippery leather soles. In the end they hired a mountaineer to do it, and, in Cleese's words, 'He ran across it as though it were a road. Quite extraordinary!'

Further evidence of the *Holy Grail*'s get-it-done-on-the-cheap limitations surfaced with the music. Neil Innes – who appears as the cowardly Sir Robin's irritating minstrel and is often referred to as 'the seventh *Python*' – wrote a few songs and hours of background music, but the lack of cash put a full-sized orchestra way out of the *Python*s' reach. Instead, they had to ditch Innes's efforts and resort to sound-effect albums and generic strings from commercial mood-music libraries.

With all of these obstacles and handicaps, *Holy Grail* stood every chance of sinking as ignominiously as *And Now for Something Completely Different*. But the sheer quality of the film overrode the barriers of nonexistent budgets and mutinous cast members. For a start, it was an outstanding piece of comedy writing. The *Python*s had taken many of the themes that had dominated their TV series and transposed them into an historical setting – particularly effective when dealing with modern stereotypes, which are made even more ridiculous when stripped of a contemporary context. Michael Palin's pseudo-political peasant Dennis at the beginning of the film is a perfect example of a 1970s shop-floor steward, farming mud instead of building cars and yet still pontificating over Communist ideology. And the Black Knight's 'Did-you-spill-my-pint?' mentality seems doubly ridiculous coming from a mythical Arthurian legend. This technique of taking the minutiae of contemporary life and transplanting it into historical settings was to bear its best fruit in *The Life of Brian* with the acutely observed squabbling of the Judean People's Front.

But if the quality of the writing was outstanding, it was matched by superb performances from the *Python*s in both their lead roles and smaller cameos (not forgetting the deftly inserted animations from Gilliam).

With all of its problems, false starts, cash-flow difficulties and personality clashes, *Monty Python and the Holy Grail* was a triumph of spirit over adversity, or in Chapman's case spirits over adversity. But the moment the film went on release the *Python*s knew they had a winner. Audiences and reviewers loved it in equal measure, and the film was a particular success in America, a much-sought-after trophy for the *Python*s after the apathetic reception to *And Now for Something Completely Different*. The timing couldn't have been better, because the release of *Holy Grail* coincided

Filming in the Scottish highlands proved mind-numbingly boring on occasion, as the *Python*s sat around between takes with nothing to do but amuse each other. Neil Innes recalls sitting in the back seat of a car with John Cleese in gently steaming damp k-niget costumes declining the verb 'to sheep worry'. Cleese – ever the semantic genius – formulated the future pluperfect 'I am about to have been sheep worried'. 'It passed the time,' said Innes wistfully.

'It's only a flesh wound.'

'Come 'ere! I'll bite yer ankles!'

with the broadcasting of the TV series on public-service television in the US, and the two events conspired to establish *Python* as an instant cult success.

The film was promoted extensively in America, and the entire group flew to New York for the premiere. Following the New York opening, the group split up to maximise their promotional clout. Eric Idle and Terry Gilliam flew to Los Angeles, while Terry Jones and Graham Chapman flew to Chicago, where they gave the first 500 patrons free coconuts. Within days, queues were forming outside cinemas and a comedy classic had been born.

Holy Grail was also a surprising winner in Russia, perhaps due to its anti-religious theme or Palin's peasant rant about King Arthur's constitutional right to assert his authority as king of the realm. It appeared that *Holy Grail* was good cinema for a downtrodden proletariat.

Importantly for the *Python*s it showed that they could function as a self-sufficient unit, without the support of BBC personnel or the safety net of an 'outsider' to direct. It confirmed their by-now-solid suspicions that, if *Monty Python* were to move forward, it would not be through the medium of television, but through the broader canvas of the cinema. And, more than anything else, it gave the group a much needed boost of purpose. Until *Holy Grail*, the group had effectively ceased to be. They were an ex-comedy group. But this film put 4,000 volts through them, and vroom – off they went. *Monty Python* was here to stay.

Python's fans crop up in the most peculiar of places – one of them dead on a toilet seat with a burger in his hands. It transpires that the King (that's Elvis, not George VI) loved *Holy Grail* so much he bought himself a copy (before video cassettes were around) and watched it five times in his private cinema. We are the Knights Who Say … Be Bup A Lula …

The stillness of a desolate, rain-swept moor is gradually disturbed by the sound of approaching horse hooves. Over the brow of the hill comes King Arthur (Graham Chapman), seemingly riding a horse. As he comes into view, it becomes apparent he's holding imaginary reins and the clipping noise is actually being made by his servant Patsy – the grotesque Terry Gilliam – clomping two coconut shells together. Arthur, it seems, is recruiting knights for his court at Camelot, and so advances towards a castle in the hope of talking to the Lord and Master. The guards deny him entry, being more interested in where he acquired his coconuts ('It was brought here by a swallow!' – 'African or European?').

Arthur moves on, riding through a village where Eric Idle is collecting plague victims. Palin tries to palm him off with an old man who's not quite dead. A swift blow from Idle's cosh soon sorts that out. Arthur is recognised as he rides past ('He's a king!' – 'How can you tell?' – 'He's not covered in shit'). He then stumbles across two bolshy mud-harvesting peasants who point out that he's got no jurisdiction over them as king because the peasants have structured themselves into a self-governing hegemony.

The king then encounters the supposedly scary Black Knight, who threatens to stop him passing in the woods. In a superbly silly sequence of gradual amputation, the Black Knight is left limbless but unbeaten ('Come 'ere, I'll bite yer ankles!') and Arthur moves on.

Meanwhile, an angry mob grabs a witch (Connie Booth) and tries to burn her, but Sir Bedevere (Terry Jones) intervenes with some dubious scientific logic. He argues that, if witches burn, they must be made of wood. Wood floats; so do ducks. Therefore, if the woman is a witch, she would weigh the same as a duck. As it happens, it turns out she does weigh the same as a duck ('Fair cop,' says Booth).

Arthur recruits Bedevere for his quest, along with Lancelot (John Cleese), Gallahad (Michael Palin) and Robin (Eric Idle). They approach Camelot, where a medieval song-and-dance routine gets underway (Neil Innes's 'The Knights of Camelot'), after which they are stopped by Terry Gilliam's cartoon God, who tells them to seek out the *Holy Grail*.

Their quest starts at a French castle, where John Cleese's iconic French guard taunts them with some of the most oft-quoted dialogue from the film: 'Your mother was a hamster and your father smelt of elderberries!' Infuriated at these heinous insults, the knights charge the castle, only to be bombarded with a surreal assortment of farmyard animals. 'Run away!' cries Arthur as they decamp to formulate a plan. Bedevere comes up with the bright idea of a Trojan rabbit,

At the opening of *Holy Grail* in New York, fans began queuing for the screening at 5.30 a.m. At many cinemas, publicity included armour-clad figures handing out leaflets and waving huge *Grail* banners.

The knights of Camelot get a message from God.

Holy Grail was 'accidentally' sold to American distributor CBS (How do you 'accidentally' sell a film? 'Oh, I'm sorry, I thought I was selling you an aubergine'). Consequently it was heavily edited and shown as the Late Night Movie as early as 1977. The *Python*s wrestled back the rights and it was later shown in all its uncut glory on PBS.

a plan which works cunningly well until the knights realise they're actually supposed to be inside the rabbit when the French open their gates.

After the first 'modern-day' interjection – the waffling historian – the knights decide to seek the Grail individually, and so begins the more familiar sketch format, with each character being given a story of his own.

Eric Idle's cowardly Sir Robin – perpetually taunted by sidekick minstrel Neil Innes – stumbles across the giant three-headed knight, and takes advantage of its internecine squabbling to run bravely away, his actions given a perpetually updated musical commentary by Innes's prancing madrigal.

Palin's Sir Galahad sees a vision of the Grail which draws him to a castle, peopled – it transpires – by Carol Cleveland and 160 beautiful girls aged between sixteen and nineteen and a half, all craving to be spanked and given oral sex. Just as Palin is about to succumb to their various delights (in a performance that finds echoes years later in Palin's *The Missionary*) he is 'rescued' by the irritatingly destructive Lancelot, who takes it upon himself to attack the women, much to Galahad's fury.

Meanwhile, Arthur and Bedevere encounter a lunatic old man (Terry Gilliam) who gives them clues to the Grail's location, and, in a *Python* scene as idolised as the Parrot sketch, they meet the Knights Who Say Ni, who send them on a mission to find a 'shwubbery'.

Idle and Chapman's stupid guards.

Lancelot manages to destroy a wedding party by slaughtering all the guests, only to discover the maiden whom he was planning to rescue is a prince being held captive by his angry father. Elsewhere Arthur and Bedevere complete their mission by bumping (rather fortuitously) into Roger the Shrubber, and returning to the Knights Who Say Ni, who have now decided they're the Knights Who Say Whup Whup Whup etc.

Arthur's knights are reunited and head off to met Tim the Enchanter – a brilliantly disguised John Cleese – who sends them to the Cave of Caernbannog, their ears ringing with the warning of a terrible killer rabbit. The homicidal bunny is eventually dispatched, and the knights do battle with Gilliam's animated creature inside the cave – the Black Beast of Aaaarrrggghhh (which is actually green).

The knights are now within spitting distance of the Grail, with only the Bridge of Death (across the gorge of Eternal Peril) remaining to be negotiated. Negotiated is the right word, as the guardian of the bridge demands answers to riddles before he'll let the knights past. The guardian is finally fooled by a reference to African and European swallows, bringing the film neatly in on itself. A tardy intermission, the reappearance of the French taunters, and then the arrival of policemen from the twentieth century brings things to a close.

Monty Python's The Life of Brian

Released 17 August 1979 – 90 minutes

I f *Monty Python* *and the Holy Grail* was the film that cemented the *Pythons* in the public consciousness, then it was *The Life of Brian* that secured their solid-platinum, gold-plated, jewel-encrusted, pearl-decorated places in the Comedy Hall of Fame. It is a masterpiece of its genre, packed with an abundance of acutely observed caricatures and held together with a stronger narrative than any other *Python* film. It also boasts some of the most accomplished performances ever from the *Pythons*, whose acting had improved immeasurably since the occasionally hammy days of the early TV shows. In portraying Brian the accidental prophet, Graham Chapman gives the best performance of his career, supported by an array of outstanding cameos, including Palin's lisping Pontius Pilate and Idle's perpetually cheerful Mr Cheeky.

There's much more to *The Life of Brian* than an irreverent look at religion. In many ways, the strength of the film lies in its combination of humour and the way in which it satirises what Cleese describes as 'closed systems of thought, whether they are political, theological or religious or whatever; systems by which, whatever evidence is given to a person, he merely adapts it to fit into his ideology'. This 'Big Idea' was widely misinterpreted as blasphemous lampooning of Christianity, and was the main reason *The Life of Brian* got into so much trouble upon its release. Never before had a comedy film inspired so much reaction from 'the Establishment' – whether it was indignation from Malcolm Muggeridge ('a squalid little film') or downright condemnation from America's right-wing Bible Belt. If a desire to offend had been bubbling up through the *Pythons'* comedy for a while, then *The Life of Brian* gave it an opportunity to surface in all its glory. In retrospect, all the fuss over its allegedly blasphemous content seems rather quaint, but at the time the conflict between the *Pythons* and the establishment figures of the day set new precedents in the legitimacy of targets for comedy writers.

The film's origins go back to 1975, when the *Pythons* were filming *Holy Grail*. Towards the end of the shoot, Eric Idle came up with the idea for a movie called *Jesus Christ: Lust for Glory*. Although the joke title was discounted, the seeds of an idea had been planted. In the months ahead – as the *Pythons* went off to pursue their own projects after the *Holy Grail* publicity tours had ended – each of them began thinking of characters and jokes that would fit into a *Python* biblical story. Although a rough draft 'of immense and complex proportions' was completed by December 1976, it would take another couple of years before these seeds germinated, grew, were fertilised, got trimmed a bit, bore fruit, were harvested and were then cut back for the winter.

Originally Brian was to be the hitherto unknown thirteenth apostle, omitted from the history books and the New Testament because his timekeeping was so bad he never made it to any of the really important events. 'The Gospel According to St Brian' would explain, for instance, that Brian had failed to be at the Last Supper because his wife had friends over that night and he'd gone to the Garden of Juran by mistake. But no matter how much the *Pythons* tried to get Brian's gospel to work, it became obvious that whenever the 'real' Jesus Christ appeared, the comedy dried up (the group had absolutely no intention of playing the Jesus character for laughs, which left opportunities for gags decidedly one-sided whenever He was around).

And so thoughts turned to making Brian a man whose life paralleled that of Jesus, but who was entirely unconnected to any of the religious or political events of the time –

Page 71 first appeared in *Monty Python's Big Red Book*, published – ironically – in 1971. Largely unnoticed at the time, it was not until the *Pythons'* next literary excursion – *The Brand-New Monty Python Book* in 1973, that Page 71 got the critical acclaim it sought. Although immediately branded a modern classic by critics and fans alike, Page 71 soon sunk into obscurity, its career halted by the public's insatiable hunger for pages 34, 68 and 111. By the early 1980s it was appearing in a number of books under the pseudonym 'Page 17', and with its career in terminal decline starred in a number of low-budget pornographic magazines, usually playing host to either Readers' Wives or, more usually, the Subscription Page.

Page 71 is now retired from show business, and ekes out a meagre living as a salmon farmer in the Scottish highlands. It refused to be interviewed for this book.

The Pythons *look smug – as well they should.* The Life of Brian *was their* tour de force.

During pre-production, George Harrison – who'd invested £4 million of his own money to get *The Life of Brian* made – brazenly exploited his status as an ex-Beatle by hinting that he and 'three old friends' would appear in the film. Not surprisingly, the media read this as a Beatles reunion and Harrison secured considerable publicity for a movie that hadn't even been filmed yet. Or paid for, for that matter.

in short, an ordinary bloke caught up in extraordinary events: man mistaken for prophet. 'Brian of Nazareth' became the new working title, and in January 1978 all six *Pythons* took off for a two-week writing holiday in Barbados, the longest time they'd all spent together since *Holy Grail*, in order to work on the script. The holiday was exactly what was needed to get the concept fully developed and dialogue polished, and the group came away from the break excited and eager to make the film (a significant difference from the onset of *Holy Grail*).

The commercial success of *Holy Grail* did not make the financing of *The Life of Brian* any easier, and a cash crisis shortly before shooting was due to begin nearly pulled the plug on the entire project. While in Bardabos, the *Pythons* had bumped into Barry Spikes, head of film production at EMI, who took one look at the script and immediately committed EMI to the tune of £2 million – the anticipated cost of filming. Unfortunately, Spikes hadn't banked on the reaction of his boss, Lord Bernard Delfont. Delfont's concern stemmed from a recent court case where self-appointed moral guardian Mary Whitehouse had brought the first successful prosecution for blasphemy in sixty years, against magazine *Gay News* (of which Graham Chapman was a co-founder) over a poem concerning Christ's sexuality. Although Jewish, Delfont felt he had a 'sacred obligation' to his Christian cinema-goers, and – undoubtedly jittery over the blasphemy ruling – promptly jumped ship.

By this stage pre-production was well under way (costumes were being made, locations mapped out, film crews assembled) and the *Pythons* were already in over their heads. At the time, Michael Palin was hosting America's *Saturday Night Live*, and he made a very public condemnation of Delfont's decision, threatening at one point to wear his Pontius Pilate costume on the show to draw attention to their plight. EMI

Brian's mother Mandy (Terry Jones) bemoans Judean dentistry.

claimed their reversal was for financial reasons – the recent hiring and firing of The Sex Pistols had cost the company dear – but the *Python*s didn't care. They had a film to make, and no money to do it.

In a typically *Python*ic twist, financial assistance came not from another record company or film studio, but from Eric Idle's mate George Harrison – one-time Beatle and full-time fan of the *Python*s. In what he famously described as 'the most expensive cinema ticket ever issued', Harrison and his business manager Dennis O'Brien formed HandMade films, and at a stroke earned themselves the titles of executive producers on *The Life of Brian*. Harrison also earned himself a walk-on part as Mr Papadopoulis, something the *Python*s could hardly begrudge the man who'd just coughed up

Still unsure during editing of how the final cut of the film should look, Terry Gilliam made several test screenings to see which version would get the most laughs. Some scenes were cut and then reinstated, some forever left on the cutting-room floor (actually they were left in the cutting-room bin. Gilliam's notorious for being quite tidy. Not 'anally retentively tidy' of course, just a tiny bit pernickety about where he leaves things).

Scenes that were permanently jettisoned included the shepherds' gathering at the beginning of the film (presented in comic-strip form in the book of the film) and scenes involving Pontius Pilate's wife (played by six-foot-four John Case), plus almost all of Eric Idle's Jewish Nazi Otto, whose brief remaining (and completely unexplained) appearance during Brian's crucifixion puzzled cinema-goers for some time. Well, as long as it took to get out of the cinema, anyway.

£4 million to make the film solely because – according to Cleese – 'he wanted to see it'.

As it turned out, the financial hiccup caused little disruption and the filming was postponed for a relatively insignificant six months – giving the boys time to fine-tune the script even further and better develop their characterisations. EMI's decision to bail out did, however, earn Lord Bernard Delfont a sarcastic mention at the end of the film: Eric Idle, strung up upon his cross as the picture fades, turns to Graham Chapman and chirps, 'I said to them, "Bernie," I said, "they'll never make their money back."' Filming got under way in Tunisia on 16 September 1978, and lasted less than two months. Instead of co-directing the film, Terry Jones and Terry Gilliam divided their responsibilities along clear lines so that there could be no disagreement as to who did what. Jones took the job of director while Gilliam became production designer, itself a massive task given the scale of the picture and the additional money pouring in from Harrison's deal. It was lucky for Gilliam that his animation had only ever been used as a linking device between *Python* sketches, because *The Life of Brian* – which was a continual narrative with little or no need for links – used virtually no animation at all. This meant that, with the exception of the opening and closing title credits and the rogue spaceship sequence, Gilliam could dedicate his time to design.

The six-month delay gave the *Pythons* time to build into the script a number of narrative 'disclaimers' which made it perfectly clear (in their eyes at least) that Brian was not a caricature of Christ. In the opening scene, when the three wise men appear at Mandy's (Terry Jones) stable bearing gifts, they realise that they've gone to the wrong barn, leaving Brian's mother peevishly empty-handed when they desert her to see the 'real' Messiah. Similarly, in the Sermon on the Mount scene, it is made painfully obvious that Brian is not Christ, who is played straight by a very po-faced

The People's Front of Judea salutes Brian the Martyr.

Ken Colley. The only humour involving Jesus is when the spectators at the back of the crowd can't hear him talk clearly ('I think he said "blessed are the Greek".')

Unlike *Holy Grail*, which was a miserable filming experience from start to finish, *Brian* was a joy. The weather – not surprising given it was Tunisia rather than Scotland – was gloriously sunny, and the freedom of a bigger budget meant that the cast and crew could enjoy some of the luxuries of a real film set. There were few squabbles and the group seemed possessed of a singular strength of purpose. All in all, the production of *Brian* was a relatively painless effort. It was only when the film was released that things started getting really interesting.

Much of the filming in *The Life of Brian* took place around the Ribat (Arabic for 'castle') in Monastir, next to a building constructed a few years earlier by Franco Zeffirelli for *Jesus of Nazareth*. In fact, many of the locations used in *Brian* were identical to those in Zeffirelli's film – such as the passageway used for the stoning scenes in both of the movies.

The Life of The Life of Brian

The stink surrounding *The Life of Brian* had been stewing for some time, and EMI's withdrawal and George Harrison's subsequent high-profile rescue had already got the public's nostrils twitching. Given the scope for difficulties with UK blasphemy laws (as evidenced by the Mary Whitehouse v *Gay News* case) the *Pythons* figured that the best way to avoid any trouble was to release the film first in the US – where freedom of speech and religious choice are enshrined in the constitution – and then sneak it into the UK. Although a good plan in theory, what it failed to take into account was the decidedly unconstitutional *modus operandi* of America's Bible Belt. The *Pythons*' first-amendment rights may well have been untouchable at a federal level, but in towns and cities across America – where local laws hold sway – a *Brian* backlash soon gathered momentum.

Monty Python's *The Life of Brian* was given its world premiere on 17 August 1979 at Cinema One in New York and almost immediately the protests started. A variety of religious factions – the ones who weren't arguing amongst themselves over whether or not it was blasphemous anyway – organised themselves into a group called Citizens

Left and top: Brian lands in the middle of a Judean Speaker's Corner – the beginning of his real problems.

Against Blasphemy and tried unsuccessfully to get the film banned. On 16 September 1979 – a year to the day after filming started in Tunisia – they marched on Warner Communications and Cinema One in New York and the *Brian* furore went spectacularly public. Over the coming months battles were fought between local censors and freedom-of-speech supporters all over America. In all but a few cases, *Brian* triumphed and censorship cases were thrown out of court, but the publicity was a bad precursor to the film's launch in the UK.

Brian hit the UK on 8 November, and already the anti-blasphemy forces had their strategy mapped out. The most vociferous critics of the film (many of whom openly admitted they hadn't actually seen it) called themselves the Nationwide Festival of Light. After careful consideration, they realised they were unlikely to secure a successful blasphemy prosecution. Instead they worked with figures like Mary Whitehouse to first ensure the British Board of Film Censors refused to give it a certificate (they failed), and then with Church authorities to spread anti-*Brian* material. But the real battles were fought on a provincial level, with local councils haphazardly exercising their right to issue stop notices on the film (a primitive but highly effective method of censorship if implemented on a national scale; entirely useless if implemented randomly, which is precisely what happened). One council, in a frenzy of censorship excitement, issued a stop notice even though it didn't have a cinema within its boundaries.

Chapman as the hilarious Bigguth Dickuth.

The net result, of course, was to guarantee the *Pythons*' film more publicity than they could ever have wished for, and, as the fuss over the blasphemy/not-blasphemy argument died down, ticket receipts just kept rising. In the end, *The Life of Brian* was as much a commercial success as an artistic one, and, in stirring up a hornets' nest of offended religious sensibilities, the *Pythons* succeeded in achieving what Gilliam described as 'a certain level of offence'.

'If we don't offend,' he said in a *Playboy* interview, 'we're just entertainers. It's one way of proving to ourselves that we're not just in it for the money.' Whether they were in it for the money or not, *Monty Python's the Life of Brian* is justly recognised as one of the funniest films ever made.

Brian Cohen – played masterfully by Graham Chapman – is an ill-fated Jewish lad who shares his birthday with none other than Jesus. His mother (Terry Jones) 'entertains' Roman soldiers for a living, and early in the film Brian's struggle for self-awareness suffers a serious blow when he discovers he's half-Roman ('I'm not a Roman, Mum. I'm a kike! A Yid! A Hebe! A Hook-nose!').

Brian works at a local amphitheatre selling snacks and titbits (otters' noses, badgers' spleens, wrens' livers, etc.). There he meets Reg, leader of the People's Front of Judea (not to be confused with the Judean People's Front ... 'the fuckin' splitters'). Reg is the archetypal union shop-steward, all motions, amendments and shows of solidarity, played to self-absorbed perfection by Cleese. Idle and Palin put in scorching performances as his argumentative sidekicks Stan and Francis. The only female member of the group (truly female, anyway: Stan wants to be a woman) is Judith, played by Sue Jones-Davis. They're a ruthless bunch prepared to slaughter any Roman who gets in their way. Well, the ones who aren't responsible for aqueducts, sanitation, roads, irrigation, medicine, education, health, wine, and public baths, anyway. As an initiation test, Reg gives Brian a job – to vandalise one of the city walls with an inflammatory anti-Roman slogan. Brian

Above: *Nisus issues Mr Cheeky with a crucifix.*
Left: *Brian suffers from bad conjugation, but he worked it out with help of a centurian.*

agrees, and that night sneaks out to daub ROMANS GO HOME in red paint on the side of a building.

Unfortunately his Latin's a bit rusty, and he gets caught by John Cleese's Roman centurion, a grammatical pedant who first corrects Brian's poor conjugations and then gets him to write out '*Romani ite*

'Welease Woderick!'

For the scene where Pontius Pilate's speech impediment is ridiculed by the crowd, the *Python*s hired a Tunisian comedian to get all the extras into a genuinely silly mood. It worked magnificently, as waves of laughter rolled through the crowd like a contagion and cries of 'Welease Wodewick' echoed across the set.

domum' (third person plural imperative) one hundred times before dawn. Brian makes off after finishing the job and the city awakes to find itself smothered in anti-Roman graffiti. Suddenly Brian's a hero. Back at the People's Front of Judea, Reg gives him a new name ('Brian that is called Brian') and then a fresh assignment: kidnapping Pontius Pilate's wife.

The raid on Pilate's palace goes dreadfully wrong as the People's Front of Judea breaks into the palace and then gets into a fight with the Campaign for Free Galilee, another revolutionary group with the same plan. Centurions appear and Brian is the only one unlucky enough to get caught. Well, Brian thinks he's unlucky anyway. His cellmate in the dungeon, Hairy Ben (Palin's 'It's Man'), can only dream of being spat at and flung to the floor by Roman centurions. He's been chained up in that dungeon for five years ('They only hung me the right way yesterday!'). As far as he's concerned, the tortured, beaten-up and humiliated Brian is one lucky bastard.

Brian is taken to Pontius Pilate, Michael Palin's speech-impeded governor ('Silence. I've had enough of this wowdy wabble webel!'), possibly the funniest cameo ever to appear on film. In one of Brian's most celebrated scenes, Pilate manages to reduce his entire Praetorian Guard to sniggering wrecks by discussing his friend Biggus Dickus and his wife Incontinentia Buttocks. In the confusion, Brian escapes and, in the only scene that sits absurdly outside the narrative framework, falls off a tower into an alien spaceship which then gives him a few laps of the solar system before crash-landing right at the foot of the palace. Like Ben says, Brian's one lucky bastard.

Still pursued by the Roman soldiers, Brian takes refuge with his comrades from the People's Front of Judea. Unfortunately the balcony upon which he hides collapses and dumps him in the middle of a Judean Speakers' Corner, where to keep the centurions off his back he launches into a speech pretending to be one of the prophets. The crowd becomes strangely interested in what Brian has to say and, as he tries to flee, they follow, convinced he's keeping some divine mystery from them. Brian is hounded by his followers into the mountains, where he disturbs Terry Jones's hermit from a twenty-year vow of silence, which he's none too pleased about. Especially when the crowd eats all of his Juniper berries.

'Yes, we are all individuals!'

The crowd decides it's more interested in executing the hermit than listening to what Brian has to say, and in the furore he escapes and goes home. There he runs into Judith and Brian forms a plan ...

The next morning Brian and Judith are clinched in a post-coital lovers' embrace. Brian wakes up, full of vigour and joy, and opening his window to get some air comes nakedly face to face with the entire population of the town camped outside his bedroom. They're convinced he's the Messiah, and despite trying to get them to think for themselves ('Yes, we are all individuals!') Brian can't get them to budge. Reg decides it's quite handy having a Messiah in the People's Front of Judea, and so gets the crowd organised ready for Brian's ministrations ('Those possessed by the devils, try to keep

Brian gets cross.

Spike Milligan's cameo in *The Life of Brian* was entirely accidental. He was on holiday in Tunisia during the shoot, and when the *Pythons* heard he was in town they dragged him kicking and screaming from his sun lounger, burnt his swimming costume, dressed him in rags and filmed him looking slightly confused as all the extras ran off set.

them under control, please!).

Brian tries to slip away but is arrested and taken to the prison, where he's issued a crucifix by Palin's social-worker centurion Nisus ('Crucifixion? Out the door, line on the left, one cross each').

At Pilate's palace, Pontius is entertaining his friend Biggus Dickus (the only other role that Chapman takes in the film), preparing to make his Passover speech where he customarily releases one prisoner of the crowd's choosing. The crowd, of course, is more interested in ridiculing Pilate than freeing any criminals, and so Palin has to run through a hilarious litany of prisoners, none of which exist ('Welease Woger! Welease Wodewick,

'Life's a bit of a shit, when you look at it . . .'

the wobber and wapist'). To calm the now hysterical masses, Biggus Dickus – who has a different flavour of lithp – steps in to address the crowd ('THITizens!'), but his attempts to offer up Samson the Saducee strangler, Silus the Syrian assassin, or even several seditious scribes from Caeseria, only make matters worse.

Judith makes it to the palace and shouts for Brian's release. The crowd love this – they've run out of Wichards, Woberts, and Waymonds – and a cry goes up for Bwian. Pilate accedes and an order goes out to reprieve Brian, who by now is strung up on his cross along with just about every extra seen in the film so far.

At the crucifixion site, Cleese's centurion asks for Brian to identify himself because he's been let off. Suddenly everyone's Brian ('I'm Brian and so's my wife!'). Mr Cheeky gets taken down in Brian's place and one by one the only people Brian stands a chance of getting rescued by abandon him on the cross – his mother, Judith, Reg and the boys, Otto the Suicidal Jewish Nazi. He's about to get despondent when – from right at the back – Eric Idle's Mr Frisbee III starts the opening lines of one of *Python*'s most enduring songs: 'Always look on the bright side of life ...'

The film ends with all the crucifixees dancing (as well as they can) to Idle's cheery ditty. Roll credits and salute a classic.

Monty Python's The Meaning of Life

Universal/Celandine Films/The Monty Python Partnership
Released 30 March 1983 – Quite a lot of minutes.

A grossly obese man walks into a restaurant and projectile vomits on the staff before exploding in a tidal wave of half-digested food and entrails. A Rastafarian opens his front door to two men who burst in and proceed to disembowel him in a lurid display of blood, screaming and internal organs. A schoolmaster teaches sex education by stripping naked and copulating with his wife in front of the class. Love it or loathe it, *Monty Python's The Meaning of Life* left us with some of the most memorable and shocking scenes of cinema. Oh, and it was quite funny as well.

Doing a follow-up to something as vastly successful as *The Life of Brian* was always going to be a problem for the *Pythons*. *Brian* had brought their unique comedic talents to a much broader audience than any of their previous work, but it was not typical of what the *Pythons* saw as their stock-in-trade – the sketch. Rather than using *Brian* as a model for their next project, the group decided to return to their roots with a film of short skits held under a single theme. And so four years after *The Life of Brian* took the world by storm, the *Pythons* assaulted us with their last and most critically contentious film, *Monty Python's The Meaning of Life*.

It was inevitable that *The Meaning of Life* would invite comparisons with *The Life of Brian*; but whereas *Brian* had a story with a beginning, a middle and an end, *The Meaning of Life* abandoned narrative in favour of a theme, in this case the superbly ambitious aim of explaining the meaning of life. '[It] had to be different,' said Palin. 'We felt we had to break new ground.'

Breaking new ground was what established *Monty Python* in the first place and, by becoming more mainstream with *The Life of Brian*, some of the group felt they'd lost their edge. Here was an opportunity to be as radical and anarchic as they wanted, without any of the constraints – artistic or financial – that had characterised both the TV series and their previous films. The result was a film that still provokes discussion and disagreement today – even amongst the *Pythons* themselves. Some say it is their finest work ever, more reflective of the true spirit of *Python* (Terry Jones's opinion); others say it was an exercise in artistic self-indulgence, or 'a dog's breakfast' (John Cleese's opinion). Others have no opinion at all, since they've never seen it (Ayatollah Khomeini).

It took a long time for *The Meaning of Life* to make it off the drawing board. An early idea was to call it *Monty Python's World War III*, an umbrella title that would bring together some of the sketches that the *Python*s had been working on as far back as 1979. But the ideas never seemed to gel together, and, as *Brian* slipped further into the past, the impetus to make the film was beginning to wane – especially since the *Python*s found their time taken up with the Hollywood Bowl Live Shows and a number of solo projects (*Time Bandits* and *Yellowbeard* were both in production during this time).

In desperation, the group sent themselves off on a writing holiday – as they had done with *The Life of Brian* – only this time to Jamaica. The first few days were far from successful, and, instead of putting the finishing touches to material already written, the group began to question the very format of the film. By day four it looked as if the project was doomed. The *Python*s were very close to packing it all in and simply enjoying the holiday. Over breakfast, Terry Jones – the dogged driver of many *Python* projects – kept coming back to the idea of the film being a life story, but he wasn't sure whose life it was. Then someone suggested that, instead of a life story, it was a story about the meaning of life. This was the spark that the group needed to get the creative engines running, and within a matter of days the sketches had been rewritten, new material inserted and the skits brought closer together under a single theme. Cleese and Chapman rattled off the opening scene in the hospital (with the machine that goes 'piiiiing') and one by one all the ideas fell

Eric Idle gives an entertaining astrology lesson in 'The Galaxy song', but how accurate are his physics? We put some of Eric's 'facts' to a panel of experts, and here's what they said:

Eric says: 'The speed of light you know, 12 million miles a minute, and that's the fastest speed there is.'

Albert Einstein says: 'Well, you're right about one thing, my boy – the speed of light is the fastest speed there is, and that's 186,282 miles a second. But that means that, over the course of a normal 60-second minute, light will travel just over 11 million miles, not 12. You must show your workings.'

Eric says: 'The sun and you and me, and all the stars that we can see, are moving at a million miles a day.'

Sir Isaac Newton says: 'Due to the rotation of the Milky Way, our solar system is travelling at about 170 miles per second. That's 148 million miles a day, not one million. Inaccurate and disappointing. Must try harder.'

Eric says: 'Our galaxy itself contains 100 billion stars, it's 100,000 light years side to side.'

Erwin Shrödinger says: '100 billion stars is a conservative estimate, but still within the boundaries of current theory. And you're absolutely spot on with its size. Good work. Could you put the cat out for me?'

Eric says: 'We're 30,000 light years from galactic central point.'

Carl Sagan says: 'It looks to me like you've unnecessarily rounded the numbers up. Our solar system is actually 26,000 light years from the centre, not 30,000. I'll give you a B minus this time, but try to be more accurate in future.'

The Meaning of Life?

'Matter is energy; in the universe there are many energy fields which we normally cannot perceive. Some energies have a spiritual source which acts upon a person's soul. However, this soul does not exist *ab initio*, as orthodox Christianity teaches; it has to be brought into existence by a process of guided self-observation. However, this is rarely achieved, owing to man's unique ability to be distracted from spiritual matters by everyday trivia.'

Harry, the Very Big Corporation of America

into place. *The Meaning of Life* was back on its feet.

Once again the job of directing the film fell to Terry Jones, while Terry Gilliam devoted his time to his own short movie – *The Crimson Permanent Assurance*. This strand was originally destined to be a three-minute animation within *The Meaning of Life*, but, by turning into live action, it grew to seventeen minutes. Although the *Python*s loved it, it simply didn't fit into the main body of the film, forcing the decision to pluck it out and run it as a separate feature. The result is clever and entertaining, as the accountants-turned-pirates from the short launch an attack on the main film. Production of the film was unlike any other, with the *Python*s enjoying all the luxuries of a grown-up film set, but without the camaraderie of a location shoot. Most of it was filmed in studios, and for some members of the group – particularly Palin and Jones – making the film felt a little like holding down an office job: turning up at nine in the morning, leaving at five in the evening. 'It was great fun to do,' said Jones, 'but it was more analytical because we were working in the studios and coming home to our families.' For long stretches the members rarely saw each other at all.

When it was released, the film made a respectable $80 million at the box office, but was met with a mixed critical response. By comparing it to *The Life of Brian* many critics did the film a great disservice, as the continuous narrative of *Brian* was more accessible and less challenging than the sketch format of *The Meaning of Life*.

For many, the real joy of *The Meaning of Life* was the way in which the *Python*s had extended their skills at song-writing. 'Always Look on the Bright Side of Life' – the song at the end of *The Life of Brian* – was a triumph for Eric Idle, who wrote and sang it (it made the pop charts and was later adopted by football fans on the terraces). But with *The Meaning of Life* all of the *Python*s (excepting Gilliam and Cleese) turned their hand to composing and lyric writing – with devastating effect.

The film starts with typically superb Gilliam animations worked around Eric Idle's insanely catchy tune 'The Meaning of Life'. Minutes later we're into Palin and Jones's 'Every Sperm Is Sacred' – five minutes of almost perfect cinema. It's a bouncy, cheery *Oliver*esque song'n'dance routine on one level and biting satire on another. No sooner has its chirpy chorus faded than we have Idle again, singing his lyrics to 'The Galaxy

Sex education – Python-style.

Song' – an astronomy lesson, philosophical argument and absurdly catchy tune all in one. Then it's Idle once more, in Noel Coward mode, telling us how splendid it is to have a one-eyed trouser snake. And at the end of the film, we're treated to Graham Chapman's priceless 'Tony Bennett' pastiche, complete with satirical lyrics about Christmas, consumerism, and the poor taste of the afterlife.

Whatever your view on *The Meaning of Life*, it was a film that marked the end of the *Python* partnership. With Graham Chapman gone, there will never be a project (in this life anyway) that will unite the six players once more. In a final ironic (and possibly deliberate) touch, *The Meaning of Life* – the last true *Python* film – ends with a television floating into view, its screen illuminated by the fuzzy footage of Terry Gilliam's animated opening sequence for the first ever *Monty Python* TV show. With the credits rolling,

The Meaning of Life?

'Remember when you're feeling very small and insecure,
How amazingly unlikely is your birth,
And pray there's intelligent life,
somewhere up in space,
Because there's bugger all down here on Earth.'

Man in Pink Evening Dress

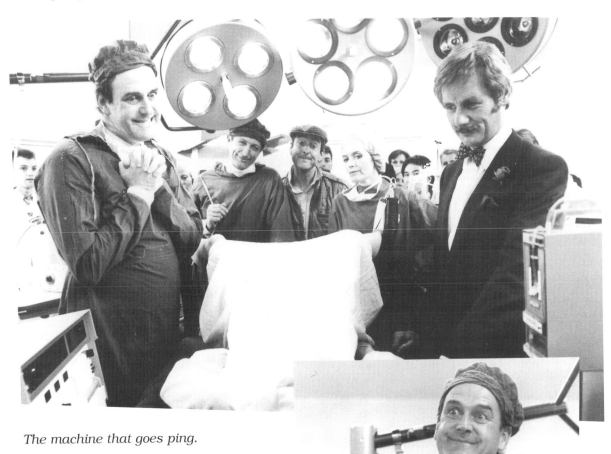

The machine that goes ping.

Monty Python's Flying Circus came full circle and ended – its place in history well and truly preserved.

The Morning Fish

As most fans know, *The Meaning of Life* was aimed primarily at an audience of fish, 'who, let's face it, account for forty per cent of all living vertebrates'. And so the film begins with six fish, whose morning chorus is rudely interrupted by the sight of fishy-colleague Howard getting eaten for lunch. Makes you think, doesn't it?

The Meaning of Life (Opening Animation)

A classic Gilliam animation (spot the visual parallels with *Jabberwocky* and *Brazil*) worked around Eric Idle's opening song, posing the terribly important question 'Are we just simply spiralling coils of self-replicating DNA?'

Part I – The Miracle of Birth

Hospital Delivery

Graham Chapman – *the* only medically qualified member of the *Python* gang – plays alongside Cleese as one of the two doctors wheeling expensive machinery into the 'foetus frightening room' in preparation for a modern birth. The mother-to-be is fortunate enough to get wired up to the machine that goes 'ping', although her husband isn't allowed to watch the birth because he isn't 'involved'. Thankfully the hospital administrator turns up to explain how, by leasing the machine that goes 'ping' back to the people from whom it was purchased, the hospital enjoys an impressive tax concession. Chapman's doctor is quite chilling.

The Miracle of Birth Part II – The Third World (Yorkshire)

Home Delivery

Palin's cloth-capped Yorkshireman comes home from t'mill to tell his sixty-strong family that he's out of work and has to sell all the children for medical experiments. The problem – it seems – is that, although the Catholic Church has 'done some wonderful things in their time', the family's woes all boil down to the fact that he isn't allowed to wear 'one of those little rubber thingies on the end of my cock'. The cast then breaks into one of the most inspired pieces of satire ever made for the screen, Palin and Jones's immortal 'Ev-ery Sperm Is Sacred', complete with *Oliver*esque dance routines and assorted papal costumes. *The Meaning of Life* was worth the cinema admission price for this alone.

Protestant Precautions

As Palin's children file despondently from the house, Chapman's Mr Blackitt – a stern bank-manager-type living across the

> **The Meaning of Life?**
> 'The world is a beautiful place. You must go into it, and love everyone, not hate people. You must try to make everyone happy, and bring peace and contentment everywhere you go.'
>
> Gaston the Waiter

Palin prepares to sell his children for medical experiments.

street – condemns Catholicism and all its 'Papist claptrap'. Blackitt rejoices that, as a Protestant, he can walk into the chemists, hold his head up high, and 'say in a loud steady voice – Harry, I want you to sell me a condom'. Edic Idle, playing Mrs Blackitt, finds this all rather enthralling.

Part II – Growth and Learning

Sudbury School

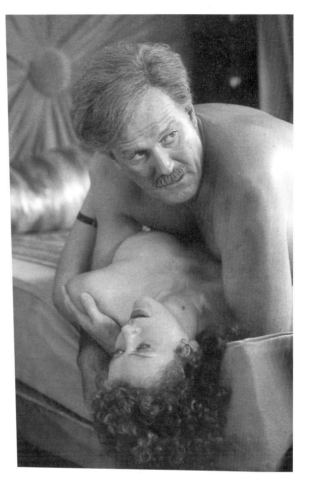

Cleese's lovemaking fails to impress his schoolboys.

It's school assembly, and Chaplain Palin leads the boys in a prayer ('Forgive us, oh Lord, for this dreadful toadying') before handing over to Cleese's headmaster, who absent-mindedly announces to young Jenkins that his mother died that morning. Then it's on to the first lesson of the day, where Cleese is teaching a disinterested and distracted class of fifteen-year-olds the facts of life. Only this is *Monty Python*, so, instead of using a badly drawn chalk diagram, the headmaster strips naked and shags his wife in front of the entire class ('Wymer, this is for your benefit. Will you kindly wake up!'). A schoolboy Terry Jones (Briggs) isn't paying enough attention, and for punishment gets selected for the boys' team in the rugby match against the masters that afternoon. He looks suitably terrified, as he should.

Rugby

Eleven large and brutal teachers beat the crap out of the schoolboy rugby team. Briggs is the sole survivor.

Part III – Fighting Each Other

Trenches

Terry Jones as Briggs again, now transformed into a captain in the trenches during the First World War, with a small platoon of soldiers by his side. He's about to take the men over the top (now if that's not an ironic summary of the film, I don't know what is) when they decide to present some gifts to him. These include an ornate carriage clock, a grandfather clock, a watch, a cheque and a cake. Briggs seems strangely preoccupied with staying alive, which the men scornfully reject as 'toff' ingratitude, until Briggs capitulates and sets up a table for afternoon tea. Not surprisingly, they all get shot. But then it doesn't really matter, because it turns out this scene is actually a film being shown by Chapman's army-recruitment general to a couple of bored-looking old ladies.

'We'll always need an army and may God strike me down were it to be otherwise,' he says, shortly before a large Godlike hand descends and vaporises him.

Marching Up and Down the Square

Palin's manic sergeant-major screams sarcastic abuse at a bunch of recruits. Would they rather be doing something else, he asks, instead of marching up and down the square? The answer apparently is yes, and so Palin dismisses the lot of them, leaving only himself to march (up and down the square).

Zulu Warriors and the Calm Leadership of the British Officer Class

Palin and Cleese are two British army officers during the first Zulu war, bemoaning their mosquito bites while Zulu warriors swarm the camp and hack their men to death in brutal hand-to-hand combat. The officers pick their way across the butcher's field to visit the tent of Eric Idle, a fellow officer whose mosquito bite seems worthy of a mention. Idle, sitting calmly in bed reading a book, explains to Cleese that the mosquito has made off with his entire leg ('Woke up just now ... one sock too many'). Army doctor Chapman (who always gets the medical roles, being a doctor and all that) makes a guess that the leg was actually taken by a tiger – the mere mention of which causes the Zulus to flee in panic.

A search party is organised and stumbles across Palin and Idle dressed as a pantomime tiger, denying all knowledge of 'creeping into someone's tent, anaesthetising them, tissue typing them, amputating their leg and running away with it'. It's a completely bizarre sketch that goes nowhere except the middle of the film. Which is quite handy really, because it's interrupted by Terry Gilliam unzipping himself from a Zulu outfit and presenting ...

A tiger alert goes out across the set of The Meaning of Life.

Only it's not a real tiger.

The Middle of the Film

Lady TV Presenter

Michael Palin *invites* us to join the film-makers in Find the Fish. Now things start getting *really* weird.

Find the Fish

Terry Jones *has* extending arms, Graham Chapman is a blonde dominatrix with bath taps for nipples and there's a green elephant-butler serving cocktails. We're asked to find the fish. Quite frankly, your guess is as good as mine.

John Cleese serves up a conversation on philosophers.

The Pythons have an acid flashback as they find the fish.

Morning Fish

If you didn't understand the last sketch – don't worry. The Morning Fish from the opening scene seemed to enjoy it, although they're a bit unhappy with the lack of 'meaning of life' type stuff so far. 'I expect they'll get on to it now,' says Fifth Fish. He'll be lucky ...

Part IV – Middle Age

Hotel Lobby

Mr and Mrs Hendy (two middle-aged American tourists played by Palin and Idle) go to eat in a themed restaurant at their hotel, a place that has 'an authentic medieval English dungeon atmosphere', complete with bona fide torture victims. The waiter (Cleese) comes and offers them a choice of conversations, including Philosophy – 'an attempt to construct a viable hypothesis to explain the Meaning of Life'. The fish in the tank get very excited, but sadly Mr and Mrs Hendy are too stupid to enjoy the conversation. 'Do all philosophers have an S in them?' asks Mrs Hendy. The waiter apologetically offers a new conversation, the speciality of the house: Live Organ Transplants.

Part V – Live Organ Transplants

Live Organ Transplant

In *the most* brutal scene of the film, Cleese and Chapman are two pseudo doctors who burst into a man's house, demand to see his organ-donor card and then eviscerate him in front of his wife. It's bloody, noisy, and very, very messy. The man's wife (Jones) seems remarkably unfazed by the whole thing, and, as Cleese flirts with her in an effort to convince her to hand over her own internal organs, Eric Idle steps from the fridge in a pink suit to sing ...

Cleese and Chapman demonstrate the dangers of carrying an organ donor card.

The Galaxy Song

On a par with 'The Bright Side of Life', Idle's halfway ditty is funny, catchy and the closest thing we get so far to the actual Meaning of Life. As a song it's cheery and upbeat, as a physics lesson it's largely accurate, and as a piece of comedy it's priceless. As a tennis racket it's fairly useless, but that's to be expected really.

Idle sings 'The Galaxy Song'.

The Very Big Corporation of America

A man paints LIVER DONORS INC. on to a wall plaque detailing all the subsidiaries of the Very Big Corporation of America. A board meeting is taking place and the chairman points the directors to agenda item six – the Meaning of Life. Harry, one of his colleagues, has some thoughts. (1) People don't wear enough hats and (2) All matter is energy and in the universe there are many energy fields which we cannot normally perceive. Their meeting is interrupted by the piratical clerks from the short feature that preceded the film, *The Crimson Permanent Assurance*, who burst into the boardroom and kill them all. And who can blame them?

The Meaning of Life?

'Try to be nice to people, avoid eating fat, read a good book every now and then, get some walking in and try to live together in peace and harmony with people of all creeds and nations.'

Lady Presenter at the End of the Film

The Meaning of Life?

'The meaning of life is a struggle between alternative viewpoints of life itself.'

A General

Part VI – The Autumn Years

Mr Creosote

If *there's one* sketch for which *The Meaning of Life* gets remembered, this is it. Things kick off in a terribly posh restaurant with Eric Idle doing a witty little Noel Coward impression ('Isn't it awfully nice to have a penis?'). Terry Jones's superbly obese Mr Creosote then walks in (to the dismay of our friends the Morning Fish) and tells maître d' John Cleese that he's better. 'Better?' 'Better get a bucket: I'm gonna throw up.' He then projectile vomits over the back of the waiter and things start getting really messy. Creosote eats the entire menu ('All mixed up in a bucket, with the eggs on top') and, after more vomiting, is tempted by the maître d's offer of one last 'waffur-theen meent'. As if you didn't know, this causes Mr Creosote to explode in 'a truly horrendous mix of half-digested food, entrails and parts of his body'. If you've decided to watch the film on video, it's probably wise to eat dinner well away from the television.

Eric Idle as Noel Coward.

Part VI B – The Meaning of Life

Ah-ha. Here we go. We're still in the restaurant, and the cleaning lady charged with tidying up after Mr Creosote has a theory. She's worked in all of the finest libraries and museums in the world, but to no avail – she's found no answers to the Meaning of Life. Now in old age, infirm and in pain, her only solace is that she doesn't work … for Jews. The maître d' empties a bucket of vomit over her head, mortified at her racism, but he too can shed no light on the eternal question of life. And so it's left to Eric Idle, whose fussy French waiter leads us (on foot) out of the throbbing metropolis, through featureless suburbs, until we come to a small cottage in the country: his birthplace. There he tells us his theory on the Meaning of Life, told to him by his mother.

Then he tells us to fuck off.

Arthur Jarrett meets an exciting if untimely end.

Part VII – Death

Animation

A trip down memory lane as Gilliam gives us an animation that could have been lifted straight out of the first TV series (only his drawing seems to have improved since then). Key characters: lots of leaves, a tree, a graveyard.

Arthur Jarrett

Graham Chapman is Arthur Jarrett, a convicted criminal who has been allowed to choose the manner of his own execution. Guilty of making gratuitous sexist jokes in a moving picture, Jarrett decides to get chased off a cliff by a gang of nubile topless models in skateboarding gear. Lucky old Chapman.

Salmon Mousse

The Grim Reaper pays a visit to a dinner party and is mistaken by the host as one of the 'little men from the village', come to do some reaping. But, according to Death, they're all victims of a dodgy salmon mousse (although Palin's Debbie Katzenberg from Philadelphia claims she didn't eat any). They are escorted – driving a Volvo, Porsche and Jensen – up to the gates of Paradise by Mr Reaper himself.

Paradise

Paradise, *it seems*, is the same cheesy hotel frequented by Mr and Mrs Hendy in Part IV. And in heaven, every day is Christmas. The party is escorted into the restaurant, full of characters who died in the film, and Graham Chapman performs 'Christmas in Heaven' as Tony Bennett. It's a great end to the film. Well, nearly end anyway.

The End of the Film Done by the Middle of the Film Lady

The Meaning of Life

Handed a gold envelope, the Middle of the Film Lady reads the answer to the ultimate question – what is the Meaning of Life? It's something to do with peace and harmony and people of all creeds and nations, apparently. She then rants on about gay presidential candidates and mutant goats, which seems a much more fitting end.

Live Shows

While *the* **TV** shows were still in their infancy, the *Pythons* put a great deal of effort into getting back on to the stage; touring the country as well as doing gigs in the States and Canada, where they were becoming increasingly popular. Maybe it was a hankering to return to the old university review days, or, more likely, because they were only getting paid £240 for performing (and £150 writing fee) per episode and they had little choice but to supplement their meagre wages with some decent cash.

Whatever their reasons, the move to live work once again reinforced the idea that this wasn't just comedy, this was rock'n'roll. The *Pythons* were doing all the things that rock bands did to merchandise themselves. They made records. They performed live; they got into movies. The shows proved that *Monty Python* wasn't limited to television. *Python* had become bigger than the medium that spawned it, and the stage work put their comedy straight into the laps of the fans. Unsurprisingly, the fans loved it.

The practicalities of getting the series from TV to stage were quite considerable – especially with Gilliam's animations, which the *Pythons* wisely decided was an integral and indispensable part of the show. They engineered a screen that was lowered on to or placed near the stage, which could show filmed inserts as well as Gilliam's links. Occasionally, they would create vast cardboard cutouts of some of the elements from the animations and use those instead, such as the enormous 'hand of God' which fingers the guilty suspect in the Salvation Fuzz – Church Police sketch, or the gigantic hammer

Mr Smoke-Too-Much live at Hollywood Bowl.

The Python*s relax between shows at the Hollywood Bowl.*

used to flatten Carol Cleveland.

The *Python*s also managed to use the audience to their advantage, integrating them into many of the sketches. The TV shows had always been filmed in front of a live audience, something that Cleese particularly found exasperating because it was rare that they actually added anything to the ambience of the sketches. Most BBC tickets for studio filming were usually dispensed free to coach-loads of blue-rinse grannies from Leicester who would turn up at the Television Centre to watch shows – any show – being recorded. It was a lottery as to which show they would get to see, and for those who ended up in the *Python* studio it must have been very baffling indeed. Their reaction was at best muted, and at times stone dead.

But audiences for the regional and international tours had invested in having a good time. These were *Python* fans who'd coughed up their own hard-earned cash to go and

The Pythons *teamed up with old Footlights chums for many of their live shows.*

see their heroes at work, and were so familiar with the sketches that the first line of a script – or even a particular costume – would often have them applauding before the sketches began. The *Pythons* turned this knowledge of their work to their advantage – getting Eric Idle to lead the audience in a rousing chorus of the 'Philosophers' Song' in the Bruces sketch or having John Cleese walk through the auditorium trying to sell his albatross in the sketch of the same name. The stage productions drew considerably on the talents of Neil Innes, much more so than the TV shows, and he became a stalwart contributor for the live performances.

In some cases the *Pythons* used the live shows to do material that had never been seen on the TV shows, occasionally using work which predated the *Python* days, such as 'Custard Pies' and 'Four Yorkshiremen' – a sketch which later became immortalised in the televised Amnesty International benefits. The *Pythons* augmented their incomes even further by recording some of these shows and releasing them as albums, notably *Live at Drury Lane* (1974) and *Live at City Centre* (1976).

But if there's one set of live performances that leaps instantly to mind – the Woodstock of *Monty Python* – it's Hollywood Bowl.

Performed in September 1980, the four concerts used material from the TV series and their pre-*Python* days, capturing the *Python*s at the peak of their popularity in the US (*Life of Brian* fever had just swept the world). One of these concerts was recorded and consequently released as a movie, and is still available on video today. What's ironic about the hugely successful Hollywood Bowl performances is that the *Python*s had really only organised the tour because they were log-jammed with the writing of *The Meaning of Life*. Frustration at not being able to get the script finished led them to thinking that a 'best of' live show would get the creative juices running and they'd finish off the

Winking and nudging at the Hollywood Bowl.

script in no time. The plan didn't go exactly as hoped, but in the process they managed to commit to celluloid a priceless record of the very best of *Python*. The all-too-obvious rush they're getting from the crowd adds significantly to both the performances and the general level of hilarity.

But the official concerts weren't the *Python*s' only excursions on to the stage during the 70s and 80s. John Cleese had long been involved in political causes, and the benefit concerts organised by Amnesty International, known collectively as *The Secret Policeman's Ball*(s) from the third onwards, were heavily populated by *Python*s. They were great melting pots of comedic talent, bringing *Fringe* players like Peter Cook alongside the *Python*s and the *Goodies* as well as contemporary big- hitters like Rowan Atkinson and Billy Connolly.

Who's Who?

That Monty Python was a collective of some of our greatest comic talent is undisputed. But what did each *Python* bring to the table? They all (with the exception of Gilliam) came from surprisingly similar backgrounds – middle class, public school, Oxbridge. But what made *Python* so special was not so much what they had in common, but what made them different. The conflict, the abrasion, the arguments: these are as much the things that defined their comedy as the friendships that have joined the *Python*s for over thirty years.

Sadly, Graham Chapman is no longer with us, taken by cancer in 1989. But the others still work together, are still good friends and are still as barking mad as they were when Barry Took first gathered them at the BBC.

Hazel Pethig, costume designer to the *Python*s since the very beginning, recalls her *Flying Circus* days fondly. 'They were always very generous,' says Pethig, 'taking us out to supper. They didn't pick and choose who they were going to be nice to – it didn't matter who you were. Whether it was the driver, the dresser, or whoever, there was no discretion at all.'

Michael Palin
A-not-very-nice-man-at-all

Michael Palin is the least likeable of the *Python*s. Bitter, angry and brimming with venom, he is widely regarding in showbiz circles as mildly psychotic and deeply unpleasant to work with.

Actually, that's not entirely true. Palin's reputation for niceness extends so far throughout the world of film and television that it's virtually impossible to find anyone who's willing to say anything less than glowing about the gregarious, cheerful, youngest (and ever youthful) *Python*. It's not a label that Palin particularly covets, however, and he's threatened that the next biographer who uses the word 'nice' will be offered a really stern cup of tea. Oh, thanks, Michael. Two sugars, please.

The reason why the epithet 'nice' does such a great disservice to Palin's comic reputation is that it implies he's boring, or not quite as lunatic as the other *Python*s. 'I can't stand it when people say I'm the sanest of the *Python*s,' he once said. 'It's a terrible slur. We are all completely mad.' But while the word 'nice' might be a gross oversimplification of Palin's personality there is no doubt that, of all the *Python*s, Palin is the least complicated. Happily married to college sweetheart Helen Gibbins for over thirty years, and father to two grown children, Palin's remarkable journey from unassuming Yorkshire schoolboy to international film star and middle-aged sex symbol is unique.

Early Days

Born in Sheffield on 5 May 1943, a late-arriving sibling to his eight-year-old sister, Angela, Palin's upbringing was unremarkably middle-class. Like many of his fellow *Python*s, the rituals and idiosyncrasies of suburban middle-class life provided Palin with a wealth of observational material from which some of the group's most enduring characters were spawned. But for Michael's family the subject of their station in life was not really a laughing matter.

His father, Ted, was a doctor's son raised in the East Anglian upper classes, and had been schooled at Shrewsbury and then Cambridge, before his work took him to India. Michael's mother was the daughter of the High Sheriff of Nottingham, and when she and Ted married it was a full society wedding with all the trappings. But the family's fortunes were then already in steep decline, and, after taking various jobs across the North of England, Ted settled his brood in Whitworth Road, Sheffield. There, in a historical note of *Python*esque proportions, he found himself working as manager of a lavatory-paper factory. When Michael was born, they were living in a rented house in a suburb of one of the most heavily bombed cities in England, a far cry from the country estates and society balls from which they had come.

Ted's sense of failure was exacerbated by a crippling stammer that made him an angry and withdrawn man – difficult to communicate with and in later years unapproachable to Michael's school and college friends. The stammer was never mentioned in the Palin household, and it was only in later years when Michael noticed how amusing his friends found the disability that he realised his father had a profound problem. Ted's stammer inspired Palin's convincing (and extremely funny) performance as Ken Pile, the animal-loving hitman in *A Fish Called Wanda*, and gave Palin the legitimacy to meet head on the critics who accused him of making fun of stammerers. Although Michael's memories are of a stable, almost idyllic childhood – albeit austere – his father's surliness cast a long shadow over his self-confidence.

Ken Pile, the animal-loving assassin in A Fish called Wanda.

Ted didn't stay too long at the toilet-paper factory (the temptation to say 'He wasn't flushed with success' is almost overpowering), and he later secured a job at local steel company Edgar Allan and Co., where he spent the rest of his working career as an export manager. Despite a very meagre salary, he managed to provide for his family and (amazingly) pay for Michael to get a private education, first at Birkdale prep school and then at Shrewsbury. For a family on such limited income, the fees were desperately high, but Ted no doubt saw that, by securing Michael's education at his old school, he was at the very least halting the decline in the Palin family fortunes.

Palin's Schooldays

Palin's *latent ability* to entertain first surfaced at Birkdale, where he was remembered for always taking the lead in form plays and sketches. His theatrical aspirations temporarily receded once at Shrewsbury, and he became a slightly more serious young man, rewarded for his efforts by being made Vice Head of House (not to be confused with the House Head of Vice, which was a different job altogether, although a lot more fun).

For a small, relatively obscure public school, Shrewsbury has a special place in the history of satire and comedy. Counted amongst Palin's predecessors were Peter Cook, Christopher Booker, Willie Rushton and Richard Ingrams, later to be the cornerstones of satirical magazine *Private Eye*.

It was during his time at Shrewsbury that Palin discovered the surreal attractions of *The Goons*, the hit radio series of the 1950s. The stream-of-consciousness comedy later pioneered by ex-Goon Spike Milligan in his show *Q5* was instrumental in the development of the *Python* format, and much of Palin's formative ideas on character and dialogue can be traced to the early radio shows featuring Milligan, Harry Secombe, Michael Bentine and Peter Sellers.

In 1962 Palin went on to Brasenose College Oxford to read history, and was selected, he suspects, because he was 'a good chap' rather than a potential academic genius. And it was here, immersed in the refreshingly cosmopolitan environment of student life, that a passion for the theatre blossomed and he met his first future *Python*.

Palin's earliest outing as an Oxford thespian was as Third Peasant in Lope de Vega's *Fuente Ovejuna*, a study of fifteenth-century peasant life

Palin won a BAFTA for his performance as Ken Pile.

written to be about as funny as an in-growing toenail. Unfortunately, there were several problems with the props – particularly a fountain that displayed a strangely human reluctance to work when people were watching, stage machinery that seized up in sympathy and lighting that worked randomly, if at all. A fellow Oxford student by the name of Terry Jones – a year above Palin – was sitting in the audience on the first night. 'It was the funniest play I'd ever seen,' he later commented.

Palin and Jones's paths would cross a few times over the next few months, but it was with fellow student Robert Hewison that Palin started his scriptwriting and performing proper. Hewison and Palin fast became friends, and under the name of the Seedy Entertainers got their first gig at the 1962 Christmas party of the Oxford University Psychological Society. Their material was a mix of television spoofs, satirical RAF wartime briefings and surreal bath and water gags – some derivative in style, some fiercely original.

Terry Jones and Michael Palin – friends and writing partners since their days at Oxford.

Palin's enthusiasm for his new comedic line of work overshadowed his studies, and as a result he failed his first-year Prelims and was forced to move out of his college rooms and into digs with an elderly landlady. In his second year – after a spell peeling potatoes in Stuttgart during his summer break – he continued where he left off, only this time paying a little more attention to getting his essays finished on time and actually working towards getting a degree. He and Jones gravitated towards each other, and together with Hewison began writing more material for a show called *Loitering Within Tent*. One of their skits – the Slapstick sketch – was so well received it was 'loaned' to the Cambridge Footlights revue, Cambridge Circus, of whom two major players had been Messrs John Cleese and Graham Chapman. This – more than any other collaboration – could be said to be the first cross-fertilisation that eventually led to the birth of *Monty Python*.

The Jones–Palin–Hewison partnership continued, first with a production called *Hang Down Your Head and Die*, and then – the biggest break for them all – The *Oxford Revue* at the Edinburgh Festival in 1964 – where Palin first met Eric Idle. Although mostly written by Palin and Hewison, it was recognisably *Monty Python*, more bizarre than their previous work and a conscious step back from the contemporary vogue for satire. It was a critical success, and put Palin and Jones firmly in the sights of the London entertainment establishment, notably David Frost, who came backstage after the show and vowed 'to get in touch', a promise which took over a year to come to fruition.

Pop to Python

In 1965 Palin left Oxford with a 2:1 degree in modern history, and made the decision to plunge into the world of entertainment full time. His first professional job was hosting a low-budget teenage pop show called *NOW!* for Television Wales West. Jones, meanwhile, had secured a place on a director's course at the BBC, and was encouraging Palin to moonlight on some of his projects, including shows such as *The Billy Cotton Bandstand, The Illustrated Weekly Hudd, The Late-Night Line-Up* and *The Ken Dodd Show.* By now, Hewison, Palin's writing partner at college, had resigned himself to getting a job in the real world, and peeled away from Michael's side, allowing Jones and Palin to strengthen their working relationship.

Palin in his first major cinematic lead as Dennis Cooper in Gilliam's Jabberwocky.

Tracing Palin's path from here on in gets fairly complicated, if only for the fact that he and Jones were so prolific between 1965 and 1967 that few BBC light entertainment programmes escaped their contributions, either as writers or performers. In one collaboration worthy of mention, Palin appeared briefly as a jazz musician in Ken Russell's television film *Isadora*, standing on top of a hearse with another up-and-coming young writer-performer by the name of Eric Idle. But the real break came in 1966, when David Frost – true to his word – recruited Palin and Jones as writers on *The Frost Report.* They joined a team that boasted some of the best talent of its day: Barry Cryer, Barry Took, Tim Brooke-Taylor, Bill Oddie, Denis Norden, Keith Waterhouse and, of course, John Cleese, Graham Chapman and Eric Idle.

The disparate talents that made up *Monty Python* were now beginning to coalesce.

'Michael talks a lot. Yap yap yap he goes, all day long and through the night, twenty-three to the dozen, the ground littered with the hind legs of donkeys, till you believe it is not possible, simply not possible, for him to go on any longer, but he does. He must be the worst man in the world to take on a commando raid.'

John Cleese

Palin, Jones and Idle were brought in to work on a children's show called *Do Not Adjust Your Set* which, although aimed at younger viewers, had all the hallmarks of pre-*Python* Python. By the second series its accidentally acquired adult audience had been acknowledged and the show was repeated in the evenings, in a new format that introduced the work of a young American animator called Terry Gilliam. At the same time, John Cleese and Graham Chapman were working on *At Last the 1948 Show*, a vehicle for the increasingly popular John Cleese, another bright young star in the BBC firmament.

The last stop for Palin before *Python* was *The Complete and Utter History of Britain*, another Jones collaboration, which suffered poor reviews brought about, believe the pair, because they were so overworked and spreading their creativity so thinly that eventually something had to give. Nevertheless, the show helped develop some of the idioms of *Python* humour (applying modern television techniques to historical subjects, for instance) and raised Palin and Jones's profile within the BBC another notch or two. It was then, in 1969, that the six members of the *Python* team were brought together under the wings of producer Barry Took to create a new comedy series provisionally entitled *Owl Stretching Time*.

Python and on and on

One of the great strengths of the *Python* partnership is the individuality of each of the members. As a group they've produced some of the most significant and memorable comedy of their generation; but outside of their collaborative efforts, each has made a successful career for himself in vastly different fields. Once the *Python* TV series had raised Palin's status that last notch on the BBC-ladder-of-importance, he was able to push ahead with other projects, almost invariably with at least one *Python* by his side.

His first foray outside *Python* was the critically acclaimed TV series *Ripping Yarns*, an affectionate and funny send-up of all the cheery shoot-the-Huns *Boy's Own*-type literature upon which Palin's generation had been raised. It was another Jones collaboration and reinforced Palin's star status away from the *Circus*. The only fly in Palin's Nice Bloke Ointment appears here, when some of the actors who worked on *Ripping Yarns* accused him of being a tyrant, but to his credit Palin simply comments that, if being a tyrant meant getting the job done, so be it.

From *Yarns* he went on to star as Dennis Cooper, the peasant lead in Gilliam's *Jabberwocky*, and later cowrote and appeared (briefly) in Gilliam's more successful second film *Time Bandits*.

After *Time Bandits*, Palin's not-*Monty Python* projects took off on a decidedly more mature trajectory, his acting becoming humorous rather than comic. His next film was *The Missionary*, the story of an Edwardian churchman returning to England after many years as a missionary in the African bush, only to be given the job of establishing a refuge for 'fallen women' in London's East End. Financed by *Python* bankroller George Harrison, it was a great role for Palin, whose boyish features and innocent charm allowed him to play the character with a charisma and sexual naivety that few could carry. The cast was impressive, including Trevor Howard, Denholm Elliot, David Suchet, Michael Horden and (personal friend) Maggie Smith; but sadly the film was not a roaring success. Even so, it showed the world that Palin's acting had more substance and depth to it than anything he had demonstrated with his *Python* projects.

Palin continued his foray into a lighter, more considered humour with Alan Bennett's *A Private Function*. It's the story of a small Yorkshire community struggling with heavy food rationing after the war, and how it secretly rears a pig with the aim of slaughtering it to provide the feast at a long-awaited (private!) civic function. Featuring Maggie Smith again, *A Private Function* benefited from Bennett's tightly written caricatures and the film was a surprising success, given its very narrow cultural reference.

Up until now, all of Palin's semi-serious acting roles had been affable, harmless characters, more victims than villains. But in *Brazil*, Gilliam's Kafkaesque film of 1984, Palin was cast

Palin's acting has developed significantly since the early Python *days, with many serious as well as comic roles –* The Missionary *(below) and* A Private Function.

Palin the globe-trotter.

NAME: Michael Palin
DATE OF BIRTH: 5 May 1943
BIRTHPLACE: Sheffield, Yorkshire, England
SIBLINGS: Angela (b. 1934)
SCHOOL: Shrewsbury, Shropshire
UNIVERSITY: Brasenose College, Oxford University (History)
MARRIED: (1966–) Helen Gibbins
CHILDREN: Thomas (played Sir Not-Appearing-In-This-Film in *Monty Python and the Holy Grail*); William (b. 1971); and one daughter, Rachel (b. 1975; played a roll in *The Dress* with Michael)
RESIDENCE: London, England

as Jack Lint, the chillingly amoral torturer who inflicts the most horrific suffering on his victims with an apologetic smile and sociopathic absence of guilt. It was a superb performance and, although the film was criminally lambasted by the critics, showed that Palin's impish features and youthful air could be applied to nasty characters with devastating effect.

Much of Palin's work has been drawn from personal experience. His biggest film success was as Ken Pile, the stammering animal-loving assassin in 1988's *A Fish Called Wanda*, a performance undoubtedly inspired by his father's speech impediment (although Palin went to great lengths to explain that his role was not a mockery of the condition). Palin had previously drawn on his own adolescent experiences to write East of Ipswich, an award-winning semi-autobiographical play detailing the curiously stifled sexual awakening of teenagers in post-war England, broadcast on BBC2 in 1987. *East of Ipswich* gave Palin the impetus to pursue another pet project, the story of Edward Palin, his great-grandfather, an Oxford don who threw away his career so that he could marry a young American he met on a walking holiday in Victorian England. It is a restrained, measured performance from Palin, and the film – *American Friends* – is an enjoyably subtle romantic comedy.

In 1991, the year *American Friends* was released, Palin appeared in Alan Bleasdale's critically praised *GBH*, as the head teacher of a school for physically handicapped children who gets targeted by political thugs after deciding to work on a day when an official council strike has been called. Based loosely on the militant council led by Derek Hatton in Liverpool during the 80s, Palin brings a humanity and pathos to the role that won him much praise. Along with numerous other film and TV projects, including the *Wanda* follow-up *Fierce Creatures* and Palin's second play, *Number 27*, he has secured a place in the hearts of the public as a versatile and much loved actor-writer. Not all of his ventures have been successful, but he appears to have learnt from his mistakes and continues to develop his prodigious talents.

And Now for Something Completely Different

There's not much you can do as a boy with a passion for trains except grow up into an adult with a passion for trains – something that often marks you out as a bit of a weirdo. This is especially true of an international film star, scriptwriter and comic actor. In 1980, Palin took up an offer from the BBC to contribute to its documentary series *Great Railway Journeys of the World*. Whereas Palin's fellow presenters chose journeys that would earn them a freebie, all-expenses paid trip between Exotic Point A and Exotic Point B, Palin elected to travel from Euston station to the west of Scotland, enjoying a brief spell as a passenger on the steam locomotive *Flying Scotsman*. Palin's episode was by far the most popular of the series, and in the late 80s, when the BBC were looking for a star to appear in a travelogue tracing Phileas Fogg's fictitious journey round the world, Palin's name rose to the top of the list. *Around the World in 80 Days* launched Palin's new career as a travel correspondunt.

It was an inspired choice. Palin's infamous niceness was the perfect foil to the (rather contrived) notion of circumnavigating the globe using only the transport available in 1872. Although it was clearly obvious that Palin was travelling with an entourage of camera- and soundmen, he maintained the conceit of man-alone-against-adversity with an acutely observational and ever patient eye. The follow-ups – *Pole to Pole* and *Full Circle* – cemented his new standing as the ironic man's Alan Wicker, and proved once and for all, as if it needed proving, that Palin is, without a shadow of a doubt, a jolly nice chap indeed.

MICHAEL PALIN

Actor
How to Irritate People (1968)
And Now for Something Completely Different (1971)
Monty Python and the Holy Grail (1974)
Three Men in a Boat (1975)
Jabberwocky (1977)
Monty Python Meets Beyond the Fringe (1977)
All You Need Is Cash (1978)
Life of Brian (1979)
Time Bandits (1980)
The Secret Policeman's Ball (1981)
The Missionary (1982)
Monty Python Live at the Hollywood Bowl (1982)
The Secret Policeman's Other Ball (1982)
Monty Python's the Meaning of Life (1983)
The Secret Policeman's Private Parts (1984)
Brazil (1985)
A Private Function (1985)
East of Ipswich (1987)
A Fish Called Wanda (1988)
American Friends (1991)
GBH (1991)
The Wind in the Willows (1996)
Fierce Creatures (1997)

Writer
And Now for Something Completely Different (1971)
Monty Python and the Holy Grail (1974)
Life of Brian (1979)
Time Bandits (1980)
The Missionary (1982)
Monty Python Live at the Hollywood Bowl (1982)
Monty Python's The Meaning of Life (1983)
East of Ipswich (1986)
American Friends (1991)

Terry Jones

Welsh, Welsh, Welsh, Welsh, Welsh, Welsh,
With a Bit of Welsh Thrown in for Good Measure

Terry Jones was born in Colwyn Bay in Wales on 1 February 1942 and, although he spent only the first five years of his life there before his family moved to Claygate, Surrey, he has always seen himself as a Welshman – a sense of kinship and identity that has infused both his work and his self-image for all his adult life. Jones's father was a bank clerk, a native of Colwyn Bay, who had to sacrifice his ambition to be a carpenter so that he could provide security and income to his family. He had a brief break from his career at Barclays when he served in the Royal Air Force in India, and resumed once the war was over, moving to the South of England with his wife (a Lancaster lass from Bolton) and their two young boys, Terry and Nigel (two years Terry's elder).

Jones is renowned for being the most literary of the *Python*s, and from a very early age had an almost precocious talent for poetry and literature (when he was six he decided he was going to be a poet, an unusual ambition for someone even twice that age). His aspirations for a life of academia faltered, however, at the age of fifteen, when on a visit to the Bodleian library he had the sudden realisation that the life of an academic was nothing more than writing words about other people's words. Jones obviously decided he had greater creative talents.

Jones went from his local Surrey primary school to the Royal Grammar School at Guildford, where – like the majority of the other *Python*s – he went on to become Head Boy. He prospered both academically and as a sportsman (his Welsh background no doubt contributing to becoming captain of the 1st XV rugby squad) and, all in all, was quite the Peter Perfect. He openly admits now that he was 'a bit of a goody-goody'. He always did his homework on time, applied himself 100 per cent and threw himself into every school activity, from rugby to the Army Cadet Corp, with boundless and irrepressible enthusiasm – a characteristic that infuriates some of his fellow *Python*s even today.

Not at This Stage

Jones was never a thespian at school. This was hardly surprising given that his school's headmaster would regularly rant about the evils of theatre, all neatly underscored with brazen homophobia, as he instructed his pupils that 'actors were by definition homosexuals and communists'. Even so, despite the fact that Jones had no outlet for his latent theatrical leanings, he was still deeply interested in comedy and film – especially radio comedy and that universal fertiliser of much comedic talent, *The Goon Show*. He includes amongst his favourites *Much-Binding-In-The-Marsh* with Richard Murdoch and Kenneth Howe, and *Up the Pole* with Ben Warris and Jimmy Jewel. He was also a film buff, and recalls being particularly taken with a movie featuring a face-pulling Danny Kaye – the point at which he claims he decided to be a film star.

Oxbridge

Like many people with literary talents, Jones was rather poor at maths and the science subjects generally. His abiding talent was a love of language, yet a silly mistake in his A-level English nearly cost him the one examination result he could depend on. He misread a question and wrote four essays on Shakespeare instead of two, leaving himself no time to complete the paper. Staying on to do a third year in the sixth form, Jones then had problems securing himself a place at university. He was turned down by London, Manchester, Exeter and Bristol, before his fortunes changed and he was invited by Gonville and Caius College Cambridge for an interview, as well as doing an exam for St Edmund Hall at Oxford.

Jones was really angling for the Cambridge position, where he was looking forward to being tutored by the poet Donald Davies. But before he was to learn whether Cambridge wanted him, he received an offer of a place at Oxford which he promptly accepted. A week later, Cambridge also came back with an offer and Jones found himself in a rather awkward situation. He'd accepted the place at Oxford but, even though it was a course he wasn't actually that interested in, he felt he couldn't go back on his word and rescind the acceptance. Further pressure from the school ensured he didn't change his mind, and so he duly started his degree course at Oxford University in autumn 1961, reading English.

It's lucky for *Python* fans that he did, because it was in Oxford that Jones teamed up with fellow student Michael Palin, who, together with Palin's chum Robert Hewison, paved the way for the success of *The Oxford Revue*. Jones says now that if he had gone to Cambridge – where the Footlights

Jones with Peter Cook, Connie Booth and Peter Ustinov.

revue was an established and well-organised entity – he would never have had the courage to get involved.

Jones always felt intimidated by the whole Oxford University experience, only realising near the end of his time there that the place wasn't quite as impressive and awe-worthy as he had originally thought. He also came to enjoy his coursework, which, although it wasn't what he had set his heart on (*Beowulf* is about as inaccessible as any literature can be), gave him a renewed interest in Middle English. It is a passion that Jones has continued into later life, leading to his publishing a serious work on Chaucerian literature – *Chaucer's Knight* – in 1977.

Jones's initial contribution to university life was as the designer on *Isis*, the undergraduate magazine. Although it wasn't exactly a satirical magazine (it had a more studious, reverent tone to it than its contemporaries), his involvement brought him into contact with the sudden influx of thespians to Oxford that year. Within a short time, Jones was actively involved in college theatre, appearing in the first production by Michael Rudman, who had started at the university at the same time as Jones.

Now calling themselves the Experimental Theatre Company, Jones and his friends staged a wide variety of material, from cabaret to Brecht. His first taste of success was during his second year, when he performed a revue called '****' at the Edinburgh Festival. It later came down to London at the LAMDA theatre and then went on to the Phoenix. Returning for his third year with the kudos of having performed in the West End, Jones immediately started work on a production called *Hang Down Your Head and Die*, alongside newly acquired friends and writing partners Michael Palin and Robert Hewison. The play was a comic look at capital punishment set in a circus ring, with Jones cast as the condemned man, a performance that earned him much praise. After an eleven-day run at the Oxford Playhouse, *Hang Down Your Head and Die* ran for six weeks at the Comedy Theatre in London. It marked the beginning of Jones's relationship proper with Palin, and in his last year at Oxford Jones took a leading part with Palin in organising *The Oxford Revue* at the 1964 Edinburgh Festival. It was a production that Jones was particularly proud of, since '****' had been very much a product of its time – very satirical and *Beyond the Fringeish* – whereas *The Oxford Revue* was far more original, showing many of the hallmarks of later *Python* ideas and themes. The then-omnipotent David Frost introduced himself to Jones after the show, and promised that at some point in the future he would like to work with the talent of the Oxford group. It was also at the 1964 Edinburgh Festival that Jones and Palin first encountered the other half of the *Python* personality, Cambridge Footlights stars John Cleese, Graham Chapman and Eric Idle.

Poor Jones

Jones's *theatrical success* was good news for him in more ways than one. His parents were not affluent enough to top up his austere grant, and so vacations were spent doing a variety of menial jobs simply so he could afford to pay his way at college. Walking the boards was a lot more fun than being a dustman in Esher.

When he had completed his degree, Jones found himself in a strange limbo, living in Lambeth but with a girlfriend in Oxford, and no idea whether to go back to Oxford and get a job or stay in London and continue with his theatrical opportunities. He made the decision while crossing Lambeth Bridge, where in an effort to snap out of an uncharacteristic moment of gloom he decided that he should start phoning people and looking for work, as well as ditch his Oxford girlfriend and settle in London.

His first job was as a copywriter for Anglia Television, but it wasn't long before he was contracted to the BBC (by Frank Muir) to do script editing and some small writing jobs. He was also put on a six-month BBC directors' course, which he was unable to complete because he contracted a bad case of peritonitis. Much to his amazement, however, despite failing to finish the course, he was offered a job as a production assistant, which he then did for what he recalls as 'a frustrating six months'. He was eventually attached to producer Rowan Ayres, who

> 'Volatile, dominant, highly energised, svelte, acerbic and coruscating are all words that Terry Jones uses with uncertainty.'
> *John Cleese*

Fishy portrait for Palin and Jones's Dr Fegg's Encyclopaedia of All World Knowledge.

took him on as a jokesmith on *Late-Night Line-Up*, alongside Barry Cryer, Robert Hewison and old college friend Michael Palin, whom Jones was increasingly drawing into the projects he was working on. Jones was still not performing at this point, preferring instead to be a much used joke-making resource within and outside the BBC.

Before long, Palin and Jones were a true writing partnership, Hewison having gradually dropped out after deciding to point his career back into academia. By 1965 Jones and Palin were contributing to a number of shows, and with their admission into the hallowed corridors of *The Frost Report* – alongside all the other future *Pythons* who were also on Frost's writing team – they became part of the light entertainment inner circle.

They were now contributing to a number of high-profile shows, including *The Late Show* in 1966. With the exception of *A Series of Birds* – a six-week show featuring John Bird – all their efforts were successful. Outside of television they wrote a highly popular version of *Aladdin* for the Watford Civic Hall. This prompted a request for them to write 1969's production of *Beauty and the Beast*.

Time for Python

Now Jones's career was really hotting up. With Humphrey Barclay's show *Do Not Adjust Your Set for LWT* – on which Jones collaborated with Palin, Eric Idle and young animator Terry Gilliam – plus *Broaden Your Mind* and *Marty* for the BBC (with John Cleese and Graham Chapman), his status as one of comedy's young guns was assured. His last work with Palin before *Monty Python* was brought together – *The Complete and Utter History of Britain* – did not get great reviews, only because Palin and Jones had not devoted enough time to tightening the scripts. When producer Barry Took suggested that this nascent group of disparate writers and performers got together to create a new style of comedy, Jones felt immediately that it was going to be a success. Over the years he is the one *Python* who has actively fought to keep group projects going and the *Monty Python* name alive.

From very early on it became apparent where Jones's talents were most effective. First, as Palin's writing partner, he was instrumental in diffusing the Cambridge style of clever verbal sketches with the wackier, more visual style of *The Oxford Revue*. Jones was very visually literate, and before long was sitting alongside director Ian MacNaughton in the editing suites, helping to give the filmed inserts a comedic rhythm and visual logic that make much of the *Python* material so durable. Initially MacNaughton was cautious about giving Jones responsibility in this area, but it soon became apparent that he was making a great contribution to the show and that MacNaughton should consider him an ally and not a threat.

The first *Monty Python* film, *And Now for Something Completely Different*, threw up some serious creative difficulties because of the involvement of what the group

Jones's enthusiasm for Python *has kept the group together for many years.*

considered 'outsiders'. By the time the *Python*s were on track to make *Holy Grail*, it was decided that Terry Jones and Terry Gilliam should be codirectors. This marked the genuine beginning of Jones's directorial career, which has spanned not only the *Python* works but also *Personal Services, Erik the Viking, Labyrinth* and *The Wind in the Willows*.

After the *Python* TV shows ended, Jones put his hand to Michael Palin's pet project, a pilot ('Tomkinson's Schooldays') for a series Palin was planning entitled *Ripping Yarns*. The pilot was a success and the two went on to write a total of nine shows over two years. Despite their popularity, however, they were too expensive for the BBC to continue making and the series was discontinued.

NAME: Terry Jones
DATE OF BIRTH: 1 February 1942
BIRTHPLACE: Colwyn Bay, North Wales
SIBLINGS: Nigel (b. 1940)
SCHOOL: Church of England primary school; Royal Grammar School, Guildford
UNIVERSITY: St Edmund Hall College, Oxford University (English)
MARRIED: (1970–) Alison Telfer (biochemist specialising in photosynthesis)
CHILDREN: Sally (b. 1974; Terry wrote *Fairy Tales* for Sally); and Bill (b. 1976; Terry wrote *The Saga of Erik the Viking* for Bill)
RESIDENCE: London, England

Kids' Stuff

Jones has an eclectic range of passions, and is undoubtedly the hardest of the *Python*s to compartmentalise. He is a much respected children's author, and has had many books published over the years, including *Fairy Tales*, *The Saga of Erik the Viking*, *Nicobonimus*, *Curse of the Vampire Socks* and *Fantastic Stories*. Many of his stories started – like the works of many great children's authors – as stories for his own children. His partnership with Palin has also extended into books, with the publication of *Dr Fegg's Encyclopedia of All World Knowledge*.

TERRY JONES
And Now for Something Completely Different (1972)
Monty Python and the Holy Grail (1975)
Monty Python's Life of Brian (1979)
The Secret Policeman's Private Parts (1981)
Monty Python Live at the Hollywood Bowl (1982)
Secret Policeman's Other Ball (1982)
Monty Python's The Meaning of Life (1983)
Personal Services (1987)
Erik the Viking (1989)
Life of Python (1990)
Monty Python's Parrot Sketch Not Included (1990)
Crusades (1995)
The Wind in the Willows (1997)

Jones's avuncular, rather woolly persona (reinforced by his casting as the 'normal' chap alongside characters such as Nudge Nudge Man in many *Python* sketches) belies a sharp intellect and breathtaking wealth of knowledge. For a year in the late 80s Jones penned a regular series of articles for the *Guardian*, covering a number of his hobbyhorses, such as nuclear power, concentration of media power, the destruction of the ozone layer (he is a committed ecologist) and the poll tax. Penguin eventually published his writings in an anthology called *Attacks of Opinion*. He is also a stalwart supporter of the Campaign for Real Ale (CAMRA) and has involved himself in a number of their projects and campaigns.

The *Python* phenomenon is proof that some of the most creative and innovative comedy comes from the measured containment of conflict. The *Python*s are a mixed bag of personalities, with Terry Jones and John Cleese representing the extremes. On one side is Cleese's highly measured and structured approach; and at the other, Jones's anarchic and random way of throwing ideas together. In working together, these different styles fed off each other and it is doubtful whether, without this inherent discord, *Monty Python* would have ever risen above being 'just another sketch show'. But conflict can only be contained for so long, and, as different members of the *Python* crew have peeled away to indulge in other projects, it is Jones whose enthusiasm and commitment to the spirit of *Python* has kept the flame alive. Sadly, with the passing of Graham Chapman, a true *Python* get-together is now out the question, but it was Jones who brought the crew together for a recent TV special, complete with the 'urn containing Graham Chapman's ashes', which was then 'accidentally' kicked all over the floor. It's precious moments like this for which we can thank the ever irrepressible Jones.

Terry Gilliam

Yankee Doodle

Terry Gilliam is a truly unique *Python*. Firstly, he's the only Terry with the surname Gilliam, something that immediately sets him apart from Terry Jones. And secondly, as an anglicised American, he's the only one who isn't British.

Gilliam's contribution to *Monty Python* is often underrated. His appearances in front of the cameras during the television series were usually only fleeting, and in the *Python* films he was always cast as unrecognisable, grotesque characters (his mad prophet and inarticulate gaoler in *The Life of Brian* are splendidly repulsive). But with his animations and opening credits he gave *Monty Python's Flying Circus* a visual identity that made the show instantly recognisable, and helped give the many *Python* spin-offs, such as the books and records, a clearly identifiable brand. He has subsequently carved himself a place as a gifted and visionary movie director, with a canon of work respected the world over – albeit with a chequered history in terms of box-office receipts.

Mini Sautéed Man

Gilliam was born on 22 November 1940, at Medicine Lake, Minnesota. He spent the first few years of his life in what was then a small rural community; a childhood very much in the style of Huckleberry Finn and Tom Sawyer – complete with dirt roads, outside toilets and winters where the temperature would plunge to forty below zero. His father had been a travelling salesman for Folger's Coffee, but packed it all in so he could train as a carpenter – a strange coincidence that links Gilliam to Terry Jones, whose own father yearned throughout his entire banking career to turn to carpentry, but was prevented by financial commitments. Gilliam's father also had an interesting distant past as a soldier who served in the last ever cavalry unit of the United States army.

Terry has two younger siblings, a sister born in 1942, and a brother born in 1950 who is now a detective in the Los Angeles police department. In 1951 his sister became ill with asthma, and the family decided to move away from the brutal winters of Minnesota and settle in California, where the drier air and warmer climate would be more beneficial to her health.

Gilliam enrolled at Birmingham High School, California (no, he's not a Brummie), where he went on to score straight As in all of his subjects, something he rather bashfully attributes to the dreadful level of education in southern California at the time rather than his own blinding intellect or studious application. But one thing was making itself obvious – Gilliam had a talent for drawing and a taste for irreverence. While his *Python* contemporaries were taking childhood inspiration from the likes of *The Goons*, Gilliam found his interest sparked by the lunacy of Harvey Kurtzman's hugely influential comic *Mad*, a style that coloured his work for years to come. Luckily the magazine's anti-authoritarian message didn't appear to have rubbed off on Gilliam too much, since he went on to become president of the student body, king of the senior prom and was voted (very presciently it must be said) Pupil Most Likely to Succeed.

Gilliam has a barrel of laughs alongside Jones and Palin.

Occidental Hero

In 1958 he graduated from high school and moved to Occidental College, where it took him a few tries to settle on the right course. Originally starting as a physics major, he then shifted to fine arts, only to find the tutor so fantastically uninspiring that he changed once more to political science. The course had the merit of being sufficiently spread out so that he was able to devote much of his time to his blossoming passion – the college magazine *Fang*. By his third year at college he had taken over as *Fang*'s editor, turning it into an unashamed tribute to Kurtzman's work, and upon graduation sent Kurtzman copies of the magazine and a request for a job. Kurtzman replied with an encouraging but nevertheless pragmatic letter. He told him work was hard to come by and Gilliam should prepare himself for the worst if publishing was really what he wanted to do.

Fortune must have smiled on Terry then, because, after a brief spell in an advertising agency immediately after leaving Occidental, Kurtzman came through with an offer. Kurtzman's associate editor on *Help!* magazine had resigned, and Gilliam was

Gilliam's first major success was Time Bandits, *starring* Python *chum John Cleese.*

given a top job alongside his comedic and publishing hero. Gilliam worked there for three years, and back issues of the magazine show that, illustrative skills aside, Gilliam had a wonderfully black sense of humour – accurate and bitingly funny – and his contribution to *Help!* was significant indeed.

It was during his stay at *Help!* that Gilliam first met John Cleese, who was on tour with Cambridge Circus in New York in early 1965. Gilliam persuaded Cleese to appear

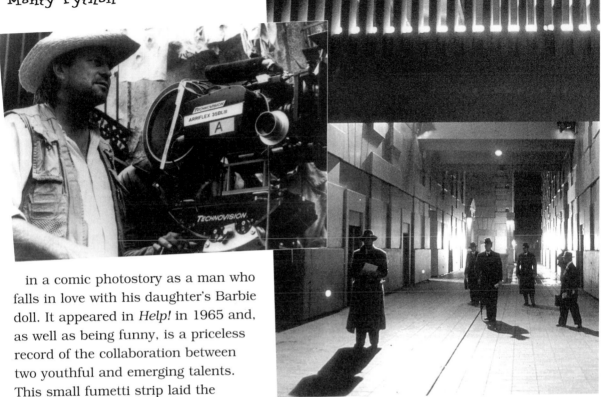

in a comic photostory as a man who falls in love with his daughter's Barbie doll. It appeared in *Help!* in 1965 and, as well as being funny, is a priceless record of the collaboration between two youthful and emerging talents. This small fumetti strip laid the groundwork for Gilliam's inclusion in *Monty Python* four years later.

Gilliam's magnum opus, Brazil.

Oh What a Lovely War!

Gilliam's bubble burst later that year when *Help!* folded. Now without a job, and with the dismal prospect of the draft looming, he enrolled in the National Guard to stave off getting shot in Vietnam. He was still required to report for basic training in New Jersey, where he had to stay for several months, currying favour with the officers by doing flattering caricatures of them and devoting most of his time to the camp newspaper. Once given his freedom, he packed his bags and went travelling around Europe, hitching most of his way around the Continent and buying a motorbike that was so decrepit and unreliable that he later hurled it off a Spanish cliff in a fit of pique.

Returning to New York after Europe was a depressing business, since he was now penniless and homeless and was forced to sleep in the attic of his old employer Harvey Kurtzman. He moved to Los Angeles to find work, with mixed results: he illustrated children's books, failed to make the grade as a freelancer and eventually got a job with an advertising agency from which he was promptly fired. At the time he was in a relationship with British journalist Glenys Roberts, who convinced him that London was a place more likely to embrace his curious talents, and that he should seek his fortunes there.

Gilliam took her advice and moved to London in 1967, taking a number of jobs; full-time on the *Sunday Times Magazine* (considered at the time an innovative publication) as well as freelancing for a few American comics. He then moved into the job of artistic director on *The Londoner*, a magazine modelled on the successful New York magazine but without one vital ingredient: success. The magazine folded and once again Gilliam found himself without work.

Disillusioned with the magazine industry (and who wouldn't be after presiding over two magazine collapses?) and in rather dire straits, he decided on a change of direction, ringing the only person he knew in television, John Cleese. Cleese suggested Gilliam get in touch with Humphrey Barclay, who by coincidence had once been a cartoonist himself. Gilliam then wrote a couple of sketches for Barclay, who, although only mildly amused by them, put two of them into *Do Not Adjust Your Set* – which according to Gilliam didn't go down too well with Terry Jones and Michael Palin, then principle scriptwriters and editors for the show. But it was while working on *Do Not Adjust Your Set* that Gilliam was befriended by Eric Idle, who helped him secure his first animation work on another Barclay production *We Have Ways of Making You Laugh*. During this transition into television, Gilliam averted a further spell with the US army after Barclay wrote a letter telling the American draft board that he was indispensable. As far as the history of comedy goes, he was indispensable: shortly after Barclay sent the letter, Gilliam was drafted into a project of a different kind altogether – *Monty Python's Flying Circus*.

What's Animation, Then?

Gilliam created the airbrushed, cutout animation style that became the visual hallmark of *Monty Python* more out of expediency than creativity. It was a 'fast and crude' method of animating that he had stumbled across a few years earlier in New York, and with his first commission for Barclay he had a budget of only £400 and two weeks to complete the job. He'd also never done a moment's animation before, and had to choose a technique that had a very shallow learning curve and could produce memorable results. His animation was indeed fast and crude, but what really brought his creations to life were the noises and sound effects, either taken from the corny BBC archives or (more generally) created by Gilliam himself. For *Monty Python*'s *Flying Circus* he usually recorded them hunched over a cheap cassette player at his desk because he had no proper studio facilities and little time to get himself organised. This was another accident of fate that gave the sound effects an intimate home-made feel and added further comic

'Some friends call Gilliam a Renaissance man; others place him earlier. The sloping forehead, the forward slant of the body as he lopes, and the prognathous jaw all point to the Upper Paleolithic period.'

John Cleese

Baron Munchausen, *Gilliam's fourth movie as director,* earned him a reputation as a production big spender.

weight to his surreal creations. The immense time pressures on making the animations for the TV shows usually meant that Gilliam was removed from the quality-control script meetings where the *Python*s would ritually disembowel their own work in a fiercely critical environment. Instead, the *Python*s would simply give Gilliam the ending of one sketch and the beginning of another and pack him off to create the links. Gilliam admits now that the murderous schedules and pressure to get the series completed worked to his advantage, because by circumventing the script meetings he was left very much to his own devices. On many occasions he would quite literally be working day and night to get them finished, often turning up on the day of studio recording with a can of film under his arm and bags under his eyes.

An Oxford Woolly

Although he wasn't an Oxford graduate, Gilliam fell into what has been described as The Oxford Camp alongside Palin and Jones, opposite Idle, Chapman and Cleese. This came about, he feels, because he was much closer to the spirit of the Oxford romanticism than the somewhat brutal and overly pragmatic attitude of the Cambridge men. This again was fortuitous for the *Python*s because it brought an element of internal balance to the friction and conflict that generated the *Python*s' unique humour. Also, as an outsider, Gilliam was able to offer a view on the world that wasn't generated entirely by the rather narrow experiences of five Oxbridge graduates and their obsession with the English class system. It was this melting pot of talents and attitudes that made *Python* such volatile and exciting comedy.

When the *Python*s made the decision to push ahead with the production of *Monty Python and the Holy Grail* in 1974, it was done so on the mutual understanding that they would take complete responsibility for their creative output – which meant one or more of them had to direct the film. This onerous responsibility fell upon Terry Jones and Terry Gilliam, who had shown an aptitude for visualising ideas with both the TV series and their outside interests (since the TV series had finished, Gilliam had directed TV commercials, filmed title sequences for a number of films and contributed 25 minutes' worth of animated material to ABC's *Marty Feldman's Comedy Machine*).

Direct and to the Point

Gilliam's experience co-directing *Holy Grail* gave him a taste of what he truly wanted to do, and set him on the path towards being the big Hollywood director that he is today. Although he relinquished the directorial work on later *Python* films to Terry Jones, he still took an active part in the visualisation, as artistic director on *The Life of Brian* and director-producer of the short film *The Crimson Pearl Assurance* which was included in the billing for *The Meaning of Life*. But it is his solo projects that have earned him his reputation as a man with a rare and unique vision.

His first film after *Holy Grail* was 1977's *Jabberwocky*, based on the Lewis Carroll poem. Gilliam was very much taken with the idea of presenting medieval settings ultra-realistically, as evidenced by the muddy dreariness of *The Holy Grail*. But with *Jabberwocky* he took this sentiment too far, and, although the film had a strong cast, including Michael Palin as the hero Dennis, and a well-written script, Gilliam's vision was too disturbing for many audiences. Despite its popularity with *Python* fans, the film only took modest receipts at the box office – a problem that has periodically troubled Gilliam over the years. Gilliam was also irritated by the American distributors' insistence on labelling it *Monty Python's Jabberwocky* in an effort to bolster ticket sales, and his attempts at getting the posters changed marked the first of his many clashes with the grandees of the US film industry.

After *Jabberwocky* and his work on *Python*'s *The Life of Brian*, Gilliam turned his hand to a second motion-picture film, this time with much better results. *Time Bandits* was the story of a small boy captured by a band of piratical dwarves who drag him through time in a series of well-crafted and engaging adventures. Released in 1981, it was a critical and financial success and instantly placed Gilliam into the Hollywood big-league. It also put some much needed cash into the coffers of George Harrison's HandMade Films, which had been underwriting nearly all of the *Python*-related projects since *The Life of Brian* and had similarly backed *Bandits*.

'The studio decided that they wanted a happy ending, which was NOT the story that we had agreed to tell originally. And so they began to cut the film. They actually took an embargo against showing the film in the States at all. So the producers said, "We've got to take these people to court. We've got to get lawyers." I said, "They've got all the lawyers; they've got all the time; they don't have to release this film. We've got to make it personal."

'The head of Universal at the time was a man named Sidney J Sheinberg. I thought, "Let's get him out from behind that corporate responsibility ..."'

Terry Gilliam on why he took out an advert in Variety *magazine to speed up the release of* Brazil.

NAME: Terry Vance Gilliam
DATE OF BIRTH: 22 November 1940
BIRTHPLACE: Medicine Lake, Minnesota, USA
SCHOOL: Birmingham High School, California
UNIVERSITY: Occidental College, California
(Political Science)
MARRIED: (1973–) Maggie Weston (make-up artist
for the *Flying Circus* shows)
CHILDREN: Amy Rainbow (b. 1977); Holly Dubois
(b. 1980; Holly played Holly Lint in *Brazil*); and
Harry Thunder (b. 1988)
RESIDENCE: London, England

The Boys from Brazil

Following *The Meaning of Life* – where Gilliam's supposed animation for the film transmogrified into a seventeen-minute live-action short and had to be pulled from the body of the film proper – Gilliam set about creating the movie rightly regarded as his *magnum opus* – *Brazil*. Years in gestation, and now widely recognised as a towering *tour de force*, Gilliam's greatest work to date was sabotaged by a Hollywood studio system that seemed hellbent on patronising audiences and refusing to release a film unless it had a happy ending.

Based on Gilliam's Kafkaesque idea of an innocent man's persecution by the State brought about because of a clerical error, the film is majestic and disturbing, a vision of a future ruled by petty bureaucracy – closely echoing Orwell's themes in *1984*. With its creaking 1940s technology, sprawling *Metropolis*-style sets, and characteristic Gilliam look and feel, *Brazil* was the film that Richard Burton's turgid *Nineteen Eighty-Four* simply failed to be. Unfortunately, its bleak ending and ironic undertones didn't sit well with Universal (the US distributors), who first believed it was too long and forced Gilliam to re-edit it, and then withheld distribution. This forced Gilliam to take out a full-page advertisement in *Variety* magazine asking, 'Dear Sid Sheinberg – when are you going to release *Brazil*? Terry Gilliam.' When *Brazil* was eventually released, no promotional funds were forthcoming and the film bombed. It was a great crime against a great film.

Gilliam's difficulties with the bureaucrats of the movie industry continued afresh with the third in his 'dream' trilogy, *The Adventures of Baron Munchausen*, a film that earned him the unfair reputation of a director unable to control spiralling budgets. *Munchausen* was certainly Gilliam's most sumptuous work to date, but the blame for the overblown budget and runaway timetable should really have been laid at the feet of the German producer, Thomas Schüly. But in the movie industry it is the director who is seen to be responsible, and Gilliam ended up as the man at the helm of a film that went on to make terrific losses. Again, Gilliam seemed to be the victim of a system that wasn't prepared to support his work, since – as with *Brazil* – little money was spent on promotion. As an example of the studio's willingness to let Gilliam be the fall guy, the distributors made only 115 prints of the film, when a full US release would need at least 2,000.

Fishing for Compliments

It *took* a script written by someone other than Gilliam (he had vowed up until then to work only on his own scripts) to redeem him in the eyes of Hollywood. His next film, *The Fisher King*, was a commercial and artistic success and, although a little too romantic for Gilliam's own tastes, brought him back into the fold. The first of his major works not to feature any of the *Python*s, it received four Oscar nominations, and secured an Academy Award for Mercedes Ruehl, the actress who played Robin Williams's girlfriend.

Gilliam's rehabilitation was complete with the 1994 blockbuster *Twelve Monkeys*, a futuristic thriller in which Bruce Willis plays a time traveller forced to doubt his sanity and eventually witness his own death. Based on Chris Marker's film *La Jetée*, it was uncompromisingly Gilliam – quirky, visually arresting and run through with a bleak humour. But it was also a major financial success and, in the eyes of Hollywood, that's all that matters.

Now with the kudos of being a director who is both startlingly original and still able to make big box-office draws, Gilliam's film-making options are unlimited. Not bad for a Minnesota lad who made his name doing farting noises to home-made animations of cars eating stick figures. Gilliam's journey through the world of show business may have been a bumpy one, but it certainly looks like he's had the last laugh.

Bruce Willis in Gilliam's disturbing Twelve Monkeys.

TERRY GILLIAM
And Now for Something Completely Different (1972)
Monty Python and the Holy Grail (1975)
Jabberwocky (1977)
Monty Python's The Life of Brian (1979)
Monty Python Live at the Hollywood Bowl (1982)
Time Bandits (1982)
12 Monkeys (1995)
Monty Python's The Meaning of Life (1983)
Brazil (1985)
The Secret Policeman's Private Parts (1984)
The Adventures of Baron Munchausen (1989)
Life of Python (1990)
Monty Python's Parrot Sketch Not Included (1990)
The Fisher King (1991)
Fear and Loathing in Las Vegas (1998)

Eric Idle

The Crown Prince of Footlights

Although Eric Idle was another Cambridge graduate and ex-Footlights president, an almost-contemporary of John Cleese and Graham Chapman, his role in *Monty Python* has always been more akin to Terry Gilliam's – a lone writer outside the parallel partnerships of Palin–Jones and Chapman–Cleese. But despite his lack of a writing partner (and consequent ally in the ever gladiatorial script meetings), Idle's contributions to *Monty Python* were no less significant in terms of quantity or quality. He is a master of language, with an unerring ear for comic rhythms and patterns, as well as being a highly accomplished musician – a range of skills that has added depth to each and every *Python* project. For many *Python* fans, Idle's songs – particularly 'Always Look on the Bright Side of Life' (*The Life of Brian*) and 'The Galaxy' song (*The Meaning of Life*) – were the high points of the *Monty Python* films. His uncanny ear for melody, combined with an ability to craft superb comic lyrics, has marked him out as a prodigious talent and a mainstay of the *Python* phenomenon.

A Little Idle

Idle was born on 29 March 1943 at Harton Hospital, South Shields, County Durham. Eric was an only child, and his mother suffered a terrible tragedy when he was two years old and his father – who had been serving in the Royal Air Force – was killed in a car crash on Christmas Eve soon after the close of the war. As a small child he lived in Oldham and Wallasey, and then spent twelve years – from seven to nineteen – boarding at the Royal School, Wolverhampton – a place that Idle later described as 'a Midlands semi-orphanage'. The school had a fearsome reputation and, although Idle claims that, by the time he attended, it was not quite as awful as its notoriety suggested, it was still an austere and authoritarian institution, architecturally more workhouse than schoolhouse. Even so, Idle, a quick-witted and intelligent boy with a bent for English, found its environment conducive enough for him to prosper academically. In 1962 he was interviewed for a place at Pembroke College Cambridge to read English.

Idle at University

As one of the younger *Python*s, he arrived at Cambridge in the wake of John Cleese and Graham Chapman, and soon decided to get involved in the Cambridge Footlights. He wrote some material and submitted it to a Footlights smoking-concert – notorious revues that were renowned for their high standards and semi-professional approach to weeding out unsuitable performers for the proper auditions to the Footlights. He was auditioned by Tim Brooke-Taylor and Bill Oddie, who must have immediately recognised in Idle a kindred spirit, since they gave him the opportunity to perform in the revue. He was subsequently invited to join the Footlights in March 1963.

Idle's ascendancy in the Footlights was swift, working alongside David Gooderson, Richard Eyre and Humphrey Barclay – who was later to be instrumental in bringing together much of the *Python* talent during the comedically fertile years of the BBC in the late 60s. But the Footlights were still reeling from the runaway success of *Cambridge Circus*, the Cleese and Chapman revue which had assaulted the 1963 Edinburgh Festival as *Clump of Plinths* and gone on to a successful West End run and consequent touring stint in New Zealand. Idle, elected chairman of the Footlights in 1965 after the barnstorming Edinburgh Festival of 64 (where he first met Palin and Jones), managed to maintained

Idle in a hirsute role for Jabberwocky.

the organisation's momentum not only with the quality of its output, but by changing the way it was operated. He was instrumental in throwing open the doors of the Footlights by allowing women to join (it seems strange today that there was a time when women weren't permitted to be part of the Footlights). As a result we have the priceless image of Germaine Greer, the fiery feminist icon of the 70s who joined the Footlights shortly after the policy was changed, doing a striptease from a nun's habit into a bathing costume and then donning a pair of flippers as if to go swimming. 'She was a very funny lady,' commented Idle (we'll have to trust him on that one).

Going Professional

As Idle's degree course drew to a close and he graduated, his stage career was growing increasingly successful. The 1965 revue *My Girl Herbert* toured Britain (at illustrious venues in places like Ipswich and Worcester) before limping in for a three-week close at the Lyric, Hammersmith. Idle had misgivings about the show from the outset, but it was moderately successful and brought him back up to London, where, when it finished, he started looking for more work. Immediately *My Girl Herbert* was over, Eric Idle and John Cameron auditioned for cabaret at the Blue Angel, and were booked in for a two-week run, beginning a stint of regular cabaret work on the London circuit that lasted several months.

Then a call came from producer Richard Eyre – one of Idle's Footlight contemporaries – who was assembling Cambridge talent for his show *Oh What a Lovely War!* at Leicester. It was a show that Idle enjoyed immensely. From there he went on to do a Christmas season in the farce *One for the Pot*. It wasn't a production that Idle particularly enjoyed, and he would spend most of his time in the dressing room writing material for the (largely ex-Footlights) radio show *I'm Sorry*

Ex-Bongo Dog Doo-Dah Band member Neil Innes worked alongside Idle on Rutland Weekend Television.

I'll Read That Again and getting berated by the rest of the cast for missing his cues.

By now Idle was putting a lot more effort into his writing and, while sharing a flat with Graeme Gardner, hooked up with Palin and Jones to write on Gardner's *Twice a Fortnight*. As with nearly all of the comic talent that was around in the late 60s, Idle soon started work on *The Frost Report*, charged with penning 'spontaneous and funny ad libs' for Frost, which led him on to scripting Ronnie Corbett's sitcom *No, That's Me*

Over There. From there he did two seasons of Palin and Jones's *Do Not Adjust Your Set*, where he met and befriended Terry Gilliam, introducing him to Humphrey Barclay and getting him his first animation work on *We Have Ways of Making You Laugh*.

An Idle Python

In 1969, as the *Python* stars came into conjunction, Idle married Australian actress Lynn Ashley during the first week of filming *Monty Python*. By now he was one of the most prolific writer-performers of his generation. During the first three series of *Monty Python* Idle still found the time to write and perform his own radio series' *Radio Five* on Radio One, a precursor to *The Rutles* – his most high-profile solo work after the demise of the *Python* TV shows.

In 1975, Idle became the first of the *Python*s to write a novel (*Hello, Sailor*) but his heart was still in television. That year he wrote and produced a series of spoof local-television shows called *Rutland Weekend Television*, with music contributions by ex-Bonzo Dog Doo-Dah Band member Neil Innes (the unofficial 'seventh *Python*'). A regular contributor to the show was George Harrison, whom Idle had met at the US premier of Holy Grail. The two

Neil Innes and Gwen Taylor on Rutland Weekend Television.

became friends, paving the way for Harrison's later financial support of many *Python* (and *Python*-connected) projects. But it was a Beatles-related sketch on *Rutland Weekend Television* that led to Idle's hugely successful cod-Beatles documentary *The Rutles*.

Modelled precisely on the career path of the real Fab Four, Idle's 'Pre-Fab Four' was a triumph, a full-length TV film for NBC with music by Neil Innes (carefully parodying

Left: *With Robbie Coltrane –* Nuns on the Run.

Below: *With wife Tania Kosevich and their daughter Lily.*

each of the Beatles' different phases) which later lead to a spin-off album. The cast included some of the comedy and music world's best-known names, from Mick Jagger, Paul Simon and George Harrison to Dan Ackroyd, Bill Murray and Michael Palin. It was shot in London, New York and New Orleans, and for a TV show the production values were surprisingly high.

A great deal of the success of the show boiled down to the quality of the songs, and as such probably represented as much a career high for Neil Innes as it did for Eric Idle. The parodies are close enough to be almost-Beatles, without ever overstepping the line, and, with George Harrison playing an interviewer interviewing a band that is effectively The Beatles, the film piles irony on top of satire on top of irony.

No More Idle Puns as Subheads

During the late 70s, Idle's career began to develop in the US, and alongside Palin he became a regular host of *Saturday Night Live*. He continued to host it up until the early 1980s. He became further involved with the contacts he'd made on *Saturday Night Live* with a guest appearance in *National Lampoon's European Vacation* alongside Chevy Chase, and then spending time with Chase writing *National Lampoon's Vacation Down Under*, which sadly never made it to the screen.

Idle was always very heavily involved in the creation of the *Python* spin-off books, and after *The Life of Brian* invested a lot of his time knocking the-book-of-the-film into shape. He also tried to produce a version of Gilbert and Sullivan's *Pirates of Penzance*, but through contractual clashes it never quite made it off the ground (a fate that has befallen several Idle projects).

By the early 80s Idle had divorced and remarried, this time to former *Playboy* model Tania Kosevich, and was directing his energies across a wide and varied number of projects. In 1981 he wrote and produced his own play, *Pass the Butler*, a terrifically weird and surreal show which covered such eclectic subjects as murder, police corruption, politics and transvestites. It had its London debut at the Globe Theatre in 1982. Although it wasn't well received by the West End theatrical establishment ('We were shat on from a great height' seems to be Idle's preferred synopsis), it has bizarrely become a cult hit in Scandinavia, where a production in Oslo has been running on and off for years.

Splitting Heirs, *1993.*

Big in Japan

Not confining himself to television, and still hankering for stage work in the spirit of his aborted *Pirates of Penzance*, Idle's career took another twist in 1986 when he played Ko-Ko, Lord High Executioner, in Jonathan Miller's 1986 production of *The Mikado* – originally set in Japan but shifted to Europe in the 1920s. He even

ERIC IDLE

Around the World in 80 Days (1989)

And Now for Something Completely Different (1972)

Monty Python and the Holy Grail (1975)

To See Such Fun (1977)

The Rutles - All You Need Is Cash (1978)

All You Need Is Cash (1978)

The Rutles (1978)

Monty Python's The Life of Brian (1979)

Faerie Tale Theatre - The Pied Piper of Hamelin (1982)

Faerie Tale Theatre - The Tale of the Frog Prince (1982)

Monty Python Live at the Hollywood Bowl (1982)

Monty Python's The Meaning of Life (1983)

Yellowbeard (1983)

The Secret Policeman's Private Parts (1984)

National Lampoon's European Vacation (1985)

The Adventures of Baron Munchausen (1989)

Nuns on the Run (1990)

Too Much Sun (1990)

Life of Python (1990)

Monty Python's Parrot Sketch Not Included (1990)

Mom and Dad Save the World (1992)

Missing Pieces (1992)

Splitting Heirs (1993)

Casper (1995)

The Wind in the Willows (1997)

Burn Hollywood Burn: An Alan Smithee Film (1998)

Quest for Camelot (1998)

Rudolph the Red-Nose Reindeer (1998)

'I don't think we'll ever escape the curse of *Python*. I feel it's like that snake with the hat on … We'd really rather hide, but it's rather a large snake.'

Eric Idle, wistfully commenting on the popularity of Monty Python *nearly thirty years after its debut*

rewrote some of Gilbert and Sullivan's lyrics (with Miller's blessing) to incorporate contemporary references to the then US President Ronald Reagan, and received excellent reviews for both his acting and musical interpretation.

In 1988 Idle teamed up with Terry Gilliam to star in the American's ill-fated extravaganza *The Adventures of Baron Munchausen*. The film was visually delightful, and Idle played his role with a touch of the old *Python* class, but unfortunately the movie fell victim to Gilliam's feuds with the Hollywood studio system and was scuppered before it had a chance to sail off into box-office history. Instead it sunk as one of the costliest films ever made.

Two years later, Idle's biggest post-*Python* film success came in the shape of 1990's *Nuns on the Run*, in which Eric Idle and Robbie Coltrane play two old-style crooks who fall foul of virtually everyone on the crime scene, and take refuge from their pursuers by dressing up as nuns. The script – by Jonathan Lynn, who also directed – is fast and pacy, and the chemistry between Coltrane and Idle works very effectively, giving Idle one of his best roles in recent years. Sadly, Idle's next film, *Splitting Heirs*, was not as well received. Written and executively produced by Idle himself, as well as featuring two of his songs, the film was too muddled to grab the audience's attention and, despite spirited support from John Cleese as a dodgy lawyer and Eric Sykes as a bumbling, useless doorman, it bombed. Idle took solace in the fact that, while *Splitting Heirs* had done badly, his most recent project before then – the hit comedy *Leon the Pig Farmer*, on which he was producer – had been hugely successful.

Idle has maintained a consistent presence in the world of comedy, appearing in a number of cameos in the US and in England. As a song writer, he is the only *Python* to have had a song in the charts: 'Always Look on the Bright Side of Life', which acquired the dubious accolade of being adopted by football fans on the league terraces. He also achieved notoriety by writing and singing the title song to one of the most successful sitcoms of the 90s, *One Foot in the Grave*, written by David Renwick and starring Richard Wilson as the miserable Victor Meldrew. Idle even made a few guest appearances on the show.

While Idle's post-*Python* career may not have been as high profile as some of his peers, he has maintained a consistently prodigious output of work, from songs and scripts to TV and film appearances. He has several projects near completion – a new book published by Dove called *The Quite Remarkable Adventures of the Owl and the Pussy Cat*, and a short 3-D pirate movie with Leslie Neilson, for Busch Gardens and Seaworld. But, for *Python* fans, Idle's place in the Hall of Eternal Sniggering is assured by the most famous sketch he's written, one of the finest moments of TV comedy ever created.

Say no more, know what I mean? Nudge nudge, wink wink.

Idle with his son, Carey.

NAME: Eric Idle
DATE OF BIRTH: 29 March 1943
BIRTHPLACE: South Shields, Durham, England
SCHOOL: Royal School, Wolverhampton
UNIVERSITY: Pembroke College, Cambridge University (English)
MARRIED: (1969–1975) Lynn Ashley (Australian actress); (1981–) Tania Kosevich (American model)
CHILDREN: Carey (b. 1973 of Lynn Ashley); Lily (b. 1990 of Tania Kosevich)
RESIDENCE: San Fernando Valley, California, USA; London, England

Graham Chapman

Gone But Not Forgotten

Chapman encapsulates the spirit of *Monty Python*: a bewitching mix of stupid and surreal, finely chopped and blended with an aromatic mixture of straight-laced and stuffy. Although he was not as prolific a writer as Jones and Palin, or his long-time colleague Cleese, he brought to the party genuine anarchy and chaos, tempered by his Cambridge sense of pragmatism and professionalism. But sadly, in the same way that the assassination of John Lennon forever silenced the discussions about whether The Beatles would reunite, so the tragic death of Graham Chapman from throat cancer on 4 October 1989 brought to a permanent and non-negotiable end the six-man *Python* partnership that had begun twenty years previously.

Of all the *Python*s, Chapman was the one who walked most precariously along the line between sanity and lunacy, a man whose surreal and often disturbing comic vision came at the cost of an enigmatic and troubled personality. Chapman was a tall, serious-looking man – pipe forever clenched in jaw – who emanated a quiet, authoritarian presence, a solemnity that gave weight to his many *Python* characters. Yet, behind this air of calm confidence, Chapman 'had a very low opinion of himself' (in Cleese's Words), a problem which led to him drinking excessively and eventually seeing his life overtaken by a chronic and disabling addiction to alcohol.

Interesting Body Parts

Graham Chapman was born in the middle of an air raid in Leicester on 8 January 1941. One of his earliest memories was being taken by his father (a police constable) to attend an air crash, where to the young Chapman's fascination and disgust he witnessed a woman walking around collecting body parts in a bucket. This experience may have contributed to Chapman's decision to pursue a career in medicine, although it's more likely that his elder brother John, who was four years his senior and had previously decided to become a doctor, was the one who sparked his interest

Since Chapman's father was a policeman, he was obliged to move around the country as his postings dictated. As a result, Graham and John attended a number of different schools as they grew up. The one that seems to have had a most profound influence on Chapman, however, was Melton Mowbray Grammar, a respected school from a small market town more famous for its meat pies than its ex-students. While at Mowbray, Chapman discovered an interest and flair for all things theatrical, getting involved in the school's annual Gilbert and Sullivan concerts, Shakespearean plays and regular revues. It was a good training ground for anyone wanting to continue the theatre at university and, having seen a clip of a Footlight show on television in his early teens, Chapman became convinced that, if he was to go to any university, it should be Cambridge. A new headmaster to the school, Mr Brewster, later supported Chapman's strategy and encouraged him to apply.

Chapman's interest in comedy was also blossoming at this stage and, like all of the *Pythons*, he was an ardent fan of *The Goon Show*, finding himself strangely in tune with the bizarre and surreal world of founder Spike Milligan.

George Harrison gets a stern finger wagging from Chapman's Colonel.

Medicine Man

His entry into Cambridge went surprisingly smoothly, after being interviewed by the Master of Emmanuel College and being told he had a secure place, A-level results permitting. Chapman got the grades he wanted and in 1959 arrived at Cambridge to start reading medicine.

Almost immediately he went in search of the Footlights, and at the beginning of term attended the Societies Fair, where all the clubs set out their stalls so freshers could sign up to any societies or groups in which they showed an interest. Chapman approached the Footlights stall and asked the club secretary if he could join. 'No,' came the curt reply. This was Chapman's first meeting with David Frost.

Determined not to give up, Chapman teamed up with fellow student Anthony Branch, and together they wrote and performed their own Smoker – 'unofficial' Cambridge reviews which acted as a first-tier auditioning process for the Footlights.

Chapman was barking mad, at times.

Chapman and Branch invited the Footlights committee, and jollied the whole evening along by supplying plenty of claret. Either the claret or the review must have impressed the committee, because Chapman and Branch were invited to audition and were subsequently elected into the club.

At the same audition was John Cleese, a year below Chapman, who by now had taken a year to get into the Footlights. They met up afterwards and went for coffee at a local coffee house, a meeting that marked the beginning of a long and successful partnership, the two working together not only on *Monty Python* but in numerous projects throughout their careers.

Take That

Their first major success was the 1962 review *Double Take*, which they wrote and performed alongside other Cambridge luminaries of the day, including Humphrey Barclay, Nigel Brown, Tim Brooke-Taylor and Miriam Margoyles. It was directed by a young Trevor Nunn, and included much material that was later recycled for *I'm Sorry I'll Read That Again* and *At Last the 1948 Show*. It was actually the last production Chapman was fully involved with, since he departed Cambridge that summer to continue his studies at St Bartholomew's Hospital.

Although Chapman was now living the life of a trainee doctor in London, he still managed to find the time to perform cabaret around the capital, teaming up with future *National Lampoon* editor and co-creator of *Spitting Image* Tony Hendra, with whom he had worked on *Double Take*. Chapman also kept in contact with his chums at Cambridge. In 1963, when the Footlights show *A Clump of Plinths* moved to the West End under the new name *Cambridge Circus*, he was called in as a replacement for cast member Tony Buffery, who had dropped out at the last minute. Chapman stayed with the show for about three months, after which it was offered a further tour in New Zealand, which meant Chapman had to make a choice between his medical career and show business. He fudged the issue by negotiating a year off college, staying with *Cambridge Circus* for the tour to New Zealand (and then an additional stint on Broadway) and dutifully returning once it was complete to finish his medical studies at St Bart's.

A Taxing Business

Once qualified, he again found himself in a tricky situation. He had earned a healthy amount of money with the *Circus*, but had made little or no provision for paying the taxes on it once his status as student expired. So, while he may still have harboured ambitions to become a doctor, he simply couldn't afford to go and do a final year's residency at St Bart's. The moral issue now resolved by economics, he turned down an ear, nose and throat position at Bart's and threw himself back into the lucrative world of show business. Work was swiftly forthcoming and Chapman found himself alongside Cleese on a number of projects, including writing for Marty Feldman's *Marty* and several episodes of the *Doctor* comedy series, where his medical knowledge came in particularly handy. He also penned Ronnie Corbett's Canadian series *Look Here Now*, filler gags for *The Petula Clark Show* and a film called *The Rise and Rise of Michael Rimmer*. But Chapman's real call to arms came when Frost recruited him for *The Frost Report*. He was to get his first proper taste of working with Palin, Jones and Idle. By the time Barry Took assembled the *Pythons* in 1969, Chapman was an experienced writer and performer with some interesting friends in the music business, including The Who drummer Keith Moon, who like Chapman had a fearsome reputation as a hard drinker and semi-lunatic.

Monty Calls

Chapman, like Cleese (and to a lesser extent Idle), was the product of the Footlights, his style very methodical, practical and professional – despite his ability to indulge in pure lunacy. The chemistry of the *Pythons* hinged on the polarity between the Cambridge crowd and the more romantic, adventurous Oxford men, and Chapman's additional bent for all things ridiculous and surreal gave the *Pythons* an added edge. His contributions were more quality and quantity, helping the others to find that single bright idea that would transform a mundane sketch into something truly inspired.

Chapman's personal life was no less complicated than his professional one. A practising homosexual since his mid-twenties, he took to his new-found sexuality with enthusiasm and gusto, becoming a founder member of *Gay News* and an early campaigner for gay liberation. But he was becoming increasingly controlled by his alcoholism, which had escalated since his days at Cambridge. By the time the *Pythons* made *Holy Grail* in 1977, his drinking had become so bad that without alcohol in his system he suffered debilitating DTs. It was not something that he kept to himself, and was as open and honest about his drinking as he was about his homosexuality. 'Drink was not always the friend he thought it,' said Michael Palin in a tribute printed in the *Guardian* after Chapman's death. 'It affected his performances and occasionally did a great disservice to a much underrated natural acting talent.'

One stabilising influence in his life was long-time partner David Sherlock, with whom he lived for twenty years and became joint guardian to an adopted son, John Tomiczek.

Dry Humour

With almost superhuman effort, Chapman gave up drinking in 1977, an experience that he recounts in his hilarious and touching *Liar's Autobiography* published in 1980. But even without the booze (at the height of his drinking he was getting through three pints of gin a day), he was a man whose unpredictability and willingness to shock made him dangerous to be around. Sometimes he pushed his *Python*esque surrealism to the very edge.

On one occasion – presented with a show-business award by Lord Mountbatten at a *Sun* dinner function – he accepted his award by crawling to the stage on all fours, clasping the award between his teeth, squawking, and then crawling back to his table. On another, he was invited to make a speech to students at Cambridge; he turned up in a full-sized carrot costume, stood at the podium in silence for ten minutes and then walked off without saying a word.

The Life of Brian represented the pinnacle of his career. As the only *Python* to play only one role in the film (bar the inspired Biggus Dickus), his acting had to be more substantial and consistent than that of the others, and he brought to the role that same quiet strength that he gave all of his *Python* characters. But unlike the other *Python*s, however, Chapman had no high-profile post-*Python* victories – no *Fawlty Towers*, *Ripping Yarns*, *Erik the Viking* or *The Rutles*, and he failed to bounce back from the typical kinds of setbacks that all of the *Python*s faced over the years.

His one solo project that did make it to the big screen was the pirate comedy romp *Yellowbeard*, a film he had originally conceived as a vehicle for his friend Keith Moon – who died four years before Chapman eventually got the project off the ground. Despite a spectacular cast, including Peter Cook, Peter Boyle, John Cleese, Madeline Kahn, Eric Idle, Marty Feldman, Spike Milligan, Beryl Reid and James Mason, the film was weakly scripted, the final product muddled and (it has to be said) dreadfully directed. Chapman was bitterly disappointed by its failure. To make it worse, his friend Marty Feldman died during the very last week of filming. The film had a pall of failure to it that Chapman found highly depressing.

Tour of Duty

One of his unexpected successes came in the shape of a series of US and Australian college lecture tours, which he embarked upon after an accidental question and answer session in Chicago plugging his *Liar's Autobiography*. Normally shy and reserved in situations where he had to give of himself, Chapman found the experience very rewarding, and the tour became an annual event, tweaked slightly so that it could embrace cabaret clubs and comedy venues as well as the university campuses. It was a shrewd move. *Python* had been an enormous success in the States, and *Python*'s perfect target market (i.e. students) jumped at the opportunity to see a real live *Python* in the flesh.

Another interest in which he immersed himself was the Dangerous Sports Club. This is the group of people who pioneered bungee jumping, hang-gliding over active volcanoes and a whole range of semi-suicidal sports activities that Chapman – rather incongruously for a public that saw him in the light of his stuffy authoritarian *Python* characters – absolutely adored. Chapman's exploits in the club included being catapulted through Hyde Park in aid of a Bob Geldof charity, and tobogganing down a St Moritz slope – something that takes nerves of steel and underpants to match. He even hosted the movie compilation *The Dangerous Film Club* and incorporated clips into his lecture tour.

Chapman's Yellowbeard.

A Tragic End

By 1988 Chapman had several ideas and projects bubbling under. These included an American comedy show called *Jake's Journey* (which he had written and starred in), executive production of the film *Love Potion*, and the ressurection of a movie script called *Ditto*, which he'd worked on with Cleese twenty years earlier and was hoping to get made. But, in November of that year, he went to his GP with growths on his tonsils and was immediately diagnosed as having throat cancer.

The disease swiftly spread to his spine, and for the next year he underwent difficult and distressing treatment. He continued working as much as he could, contributing to *Parrot Sketch Not Included* and *The Movie Life of George*, but in September of 1989 he was rushed into hospital and the cancer was pronounced incurable. His family and friends gathered round him, and Chapman passed away on 4 October 1989, with (amongst others) Cleese and Palin by his side.

The next day, 5 October, had been planned as a huge celebration of twenty years of *Monty Python* (the first episode was recorded on 5 October 1969) and Chapman's death – in an instance of *Python*esque timing – meant the party had to be postponed. 'It was,' said Terry Jones, 'the worst case of party-pooping I've ever seen.' The *Python*s chose to stay away from Chapman's funeral, wisely deciding that it would be intrusive for his family if it turned into a show-business gathering. Instead, they sent a floral wreath (in

NAME: Graham Chapman
DATE OF BIRTH: 8 January 1941
DIED: 4 October 1989 (Graham died as a result of cancer of the larynx)
BIRTHPLACE: Leicester, Midlands, England
SIBLINGS: John (b. 1937; a doctor, in whose footsteps Graham wanted to follow)
SCHOOL: Melton Mowbray Grammar
UNIVERSITY: Emmanuel College, Cambridge University (Medicine)
MARRIED: Lived with his lover, David Sherlock, until his death in 1989
CHILDREN: Graham and David adopted a son, John Tomiczek, in 1971. John died in 1992

the shape of a *Python*esque foot) bearing the inscription 'To Graham from the other *Python*s. Stop us if we're getting too silly'. They also organised a memorial service held two months after his death at St Bart's Hospital Great Hall.

At the memorial, Eric Idle led a rousing chorus of 'Always Look on the Bright Side of Life', then John Cleese addressed the congregation to say that 'Graham Chapman is no more. He has gone to meet his maker. He has run down the curtain and joined the choir invisible.' Cleese finished by claiming to be the first person to say 'fuck' at a memorial service. Then the Fred Tomlinson singers led the congregation in a chorus of 'Jerusalem' in Japanese (or 'Jelusarem', as Chapman preferred) with the lines: 'Bling me my speal, oh crowds unford, Bling me my chaliots of file ...'

GRAHAM CHAPMAN
How to Irritate People (1968)
And Now for Something Completely Different (1972)
Monty Python and the Holy Grail (1975)
The Odd Job (1978)
Monty Python's Life of Brian (1979)
The Secret Policeman's Other Ball (1982)
Monty Python Live at the Hollywood Bowl (1982)
Yellowbeard (1983)
Monty Python's The Meaning of Life (1983)
The Secret Policeman's Private Parts (1984)
Monty Python's Parrot Sketch Not Included (1990)
Life of Python (1990)

Each of the *Python*s, and many of Chapman's old friends from the Footlights days, paid their respects or contributed to the service. Notable was Eric Idle's address, in which, choking back the tears, he said that Chapman always thought Palin talked too much and had died rather than listen to him any more.

It was a poignant and *Python*esque send-off to the man who, so comfortable flirting with lunacy himself, had introduced its sublime charms to the world through the madness of *Monty Python*.

John Cleese

John Cleese is arguably the finest British comedy actor of his generation. As both a writer and performer he has succeeded in encapsulating everything that's odd about being an Englishman; about being part of a parochial class system; about being emotionally and sexually repressed; about being uptight, uncomfortable and uncommunicative. In short (or, in his case, in tall), he has come to represent the English Woody Allen – full of neuroses but too emotionally inarticulate to express them. Through *Monty Python*, *Fawlty Towers*, *A Fish Called Wanda* and his innumerable other film and television roles, he has reached that curiously untouchable status of entertainment demigod. But he is also a man of great internal discord, something of a cold fish who has struggled throughout his career to find peace as much as he has sought success. Complicated, irascible, stubborn, manipulative and possessed of a genuine comic genius, John Cleese is the man without whom the whole *Monty Python* phenomenon would simply not have happened. And he very nearly spent his life as a solicitor.

John Marwood Cleese was born on 27 October 1939 in Weston-Super-Mare, a coastal 'resort' that has the dubious distinction of having one of the muddiest and smelliest beaches in England. He was a late arrival to his father and mother, who at the time of his birth were 46 and 40 years old respectively and had been married for thirteen years. He grew up with elderly, overly protective parents, and was mollycoddled to the extent that as a boy he wasn't even allowed a bicycle in case he hurt himself.

His father, Reg, was an averagely paid insurance salesman who had fought in the First World War, and who up until his army days was actually called Reg Cheese. Anticipating a barrage of barracks jokes regarding his name, he had it legally changed to Cleese shortly before signing up – so saving himself (and later his son) from the tiresome business of smiling politely at cheese jokes.

Streak of Bacon

That John Cleese is a tall man (six foot five at the last count) is beyond any shadow of a doubt. But his gangly height is so caricatured in our consciousness as the Minister for Silly Walks and the lunging, flailing Basil Fawlty that we sometimes forget that the caricature is actually a real person. By the time he was twelve, Cleese was already six foot and, since he was a very meek and mild-mannered boy, it made him an easy target for school bullies and sarcastic teachers. Like many comedians and comic actors, Cleese recalls that his humour developed as a self-defence mechanism, a way to diffuse harassment by making his persecutors laugh instead of him having to hit them back. With his quick wit and sophisticated sense of humour, it became an

easy way for Cleese to make himself liked – although later in life he has been very self-deprecating about his popularity at school.

Cleese's father was an unassertive man, kindly and overindulgent, who never chastised John and would go to great lengths to quell his temper – a peculiarly English trait that surfaces time and time again in Cleese's work. As an adult, the subject of suppressed anger was one that fascinated him both

Cleese's second brush with the legal profession in A Fish called Wanda.

personally and professionally for many years, and the wincing, teeth grinding Basil Fawlty can be traced directly to Cleese's obsession with the very middle-class affectation of avoiding scenes and arguments.

As with Michael Palin, Cleese's father struggled hard to find the money to send him to private school, but find it he did. Cleese was sent first to St Peter's Prep School and then – at the age of fourteen – Clifton College, where he was again singled out, this time as one of only a few day boys in a school geared largely towards the boarders. Always the 'odd one out', Cleese was already displaying signs of a precocious and deeply subversive sense of humour. In his excellent and thoroughly well-researched biography, Jonathan Margolis recounts an episode told by one of Cleese's contemporaries at St Peter's. One of his teachers, a short man by the name of Milligan, had lined up Cleese's class in a corridor prior to lunch, with the aim of ensuring they'd all washed their hands. Cleese, already six foot and towering over the diminutive teacher, turned to him as he was checking the boys' hands and said, 'You know, sir, I've been thinking about something.' 'And what is that, Cleese?' 'A milligram is a very small thing,' replied the deadpan Cleese. Milligan, of course, was livid, but Cleese had wrapped up his insult so well that the teacher was powerless to unpick it.

At Clifton, Cleese was academically successful, winning a scholarship for

mathematics, and was adept at English and Latin, although he eventually went on to take A levels in maths, physics and chemistry. He was also quite sporty, playing football for the school team as well as cricket, where he ended up reaching the First XI and playing several matches at Lord's on behalf of the school.

Even as a boy, Cleese had an interest in writing sketches and comic dialogues, inspired by the radio show *Up the Pole* and later – like all the *Python*s – by *The Goon Show*. Cleese was articulate and verbally dextrous, quick to find weaknesses in others' arguments and adept at using his writing skills in all manner of situations (he won the Twelve and Over Writing Competition at St Peter's in 1951). He was also starting to flex his muscles in terms of performing, appearing in a few school plays and doing a Flanders and Swann routine for a revue.

Legal Beagle

In 1958 Cleese passed the exam that secured him a place at Downing College Cambridge to read law, although his preferred choice was Pembroke (Eric Idle would later recall that Cleese spent so much time hanging around Pembroke anyway that all the masters thought he was a Pembroke student). Law was chosen not because he had a burning ambition to be a barrister, but because he was aware that the legal profession had cropped up somewhere in the family history (it later turned out his grandfather had been a solicitor's clerk). He also felt that his talent for semantics would stand him in good stead in a profession that was essentially all about the logic of language and argument.

But Cleese's plans were to be disrupted by the termination of National Service, when the sudden influx of students entering the university system, having postponed their degree courses, meant that Cleese had to wait two years before he could take his place. Hence the fact that, although two years older than Graham Chapman, he was a year below at Cambridge.

To fill the time he (rather unambitiously) went back to his old preparatory school to teach, something that he found greatly enjoyable. Cleese has said since that if he hadn't been successful as a comic actor, he would have been quite happy to go back into teaching full time. Seeing his schoolmaster's performances in *Clockwise* and *The Meaning of Life*, it's all too easy to imagine him stalking school corridors in a mortarboard and cape, quelling childish anarchy with well-timed acerbic barks.

Cleese took his place at Cambridge in 1960, and straight away homed in on the Footlights. A law student armed with science A levels, he was immediately at a disadvantage trying to enter a club dominated by Arts students. His first approach to the club was rather lame, having to admit that he couldn't sing, couldn't dance, and saying rather apologetically that his thing was 'trying to make people laugh'. He was, naturally, rebuffed, and it wasn't until his second term, when he teamed up with fellow undergraduate Alan Hutchison, that he found a way in. Hutchison was a friend of the Footlights treasurer, and through this contact Cleese submitted material that was eventually used in the 1961 revue *I Thought I Saw It Move* (headlined by a young and dangerously ambitious David Frost), which led to him and Hutchison getting elected. At the audition, Cleese met Graham Chapman, a medical student a year above him, and the two immediately started working on scripts together.

Cleese moved into digs just round the corner from the Footlights club room (a newly acquired venue that had previously been the HQ of the Cambridge University Labour Club) and began hanging around with future Goodies Tim Brooke-Taylor and Bill Oddie. He was now spending time with his new writing partner, Chapman, and the two performed together for the first time in 1962's *Double Take*, after which Chapman went to St Bart's Hospital to study and Cleese became instrumental in the following year's revue, *A Clump of Plinths* (later changed to *Cambridge Circus*). In amongst all of this, Cleese still found the time to pass his law exams with a very respectable 2:1.

'I wanna hold your hand!'

Circus Performer

Cleese seems to have been wrong-footed by the sudden success of *Cambridge Circus*. In a matter of weeks he'd gone from accepting a post at a solicitor's firm in the City to being offered a job at the BBC as a scriptwriter-editor and having his revue signed up for a run in the West End. He accepted the job at the BBC, where he wrote for a number of pilots and existing programmes, including the *Dick Emery Show*. But in 1964 he put the job on ice when offered the chance to rejoin *Cambridge Circus* on a tour of New Zealand and then Broadway, where he met wife-to-be Connie Booth, who was waitressing in a New York diner (they married in 1968).

After the show ended, Cleese stayed on in New York to appear in the US production of *Half a Sixpence*, as the man who embezzles Tommy Steele's recently acquired wealth. Although it was a musical, the director allowed Cleese to mime all his chorus-line appearances because he was such a terrible singer – praise indeed for the comic talents, that made up for this shortcoming. Cleese stayed in the States for some time, doing a number of different jobs, ranging from serious journalism on *Newsweek* to playing in the *American Establishment Review* in Chicago and Washington. He also met American comic artist Terry Gilliam, who recruited him to appear in a humorous photostory for his magazine *Help!*

On returning to England in Christmas 1965, Cleese was immediately snapped up by the magpie-like David Frost, who had an eye for collecting all the glittering talent of the day to work on his *Frost Report* television show. It was here that Cleese was teamed up with Graham Chapman again, and worked for the first time with fellow *Python*s Eric Idle, Michael Palin and Terry Jones. Cleese also performed on the show in a number of memorable sketches, such as the upper-middle-lower class skit featuring Ronnie Corbett and Ronnie Barker. He also started writing and performing for the radio show *I'm Sorry I'll Read That Again.*

Ronnie Corbett and John Cleese team up on The Frost Report.

Cleese the Achiever

By the late 60s Cleese's litany of contributions was tomelike. From the TV work of *At Last the 1948 Show*, *Doctor in the House* and *Marty* to films such as *The Rise and Rise of Michael Rimmer*, *Rentadick* and *The Best House of London*, he was one of the BBC's hottest young talents.

When the *Python*s were assembled in 1969, it was an open secret around the halls

With Alyce Faye Eichelberger and daughter Cynthia.

of the corporation that it was primarily a vehicle for John Cleese, and that, without his presence, *Monty Python* would never have come into being. But it became immediately obvious to Barry Took and others that Cleese had been teamed up with a bunch of similarly talented writer-performers, and there was not a passenger amongst them. But Cleese was still the power broker, and for a long time he was the one who took notional charge of script meetings, rehearsals and liaison with the BBC management.

Cleese found *Python* hugely liberating: after his time spent writing material around the constraints of other shows, here was an opportunity to do whatever he wanted within the confines of BBC policy. His influence in the group dynamics was as a constantly disapproving schoolmaster, forever driving himself and his colleagues to be frank about their work (bordering on the rude), and never shying away from telling others what he thought of a sketch or a joke. He was quite abrasive, and often found himself at complete loggerheads with his *Python* antithesis, Terry Jones, who favoured a laid-back and less judgmental approach. Cleese was a self-confessed 'compulsive perfectionist' and even his writing partner Chapman found the endless rewrites and edits and tweaks and fine-tuning to be infuriating.

Of the other *Python*s, Cleese was most impressed with Palin, and tried for a while to swap the writing partnerships around so that the chemistry of the group could undergo change (for no reason other than that he thought change was a good thing). It was a short-lived experiment that led to him and Palin writing the North Minehead By-Election

Above: At Last the 1948 Show.

Below: *Another of Cleese's authority figures bullies Jones's old lady.*

sketch, and Idle and Cleese penning the Sir George Head mountaineering sketch ('To the twin peaks of Kilimanjaro'). But, writing partners aside, for Cleese the constant source of inspiration for his comedy was the authority figure – the policeman, the civil servant, the accountant. These were the characters he most cruelly caricatured, possibly because these were the figures with which he most closely identified. There's much truth in the adage that we despise most those people who reflect the qualities we dislike in ourselves, and Cleese – who later in life was very honest about his experiences at the hands of a psychoanalyst – no doubt fuelled his comedy with a deep understanding of the authority figures he satirised.

JOHN CLEESE
Actor
Interlude (1968)
The Bliss of Mrs Blossom (1968)
The Magic Christian (1969)
The Best House in London (1969)
The Statue (1971)
And Now for Something Completely Different (1971)
The Love Ban (1973)
Monty Python and the Holy Grail (1974)
Romance with a Double Bass (1974)
Monty Python Meets Beyond the Fringe (1977)
The Strange Case of the End of Civilisation as We Know It (1977)
Life of Brian (1979)
Time Bandits (1980)
The Great Muppet Caper (1981)
The Secret Policeman's Ball (1981)
Monty Python Live at the Hollywood Bowl (1982)
Privates on Parade (1982)
The Secret Policeman's Other Ball (1982)
Monty Python's the Meaning of Life (1983)
Yellowbeard (1983)
The Secret Policeman's Private Parts (1984)
Silverado (1985)
Clockwise (1986)
A Fish Called Wanda (1988)
The Big Picture (1989)
Erik the Viking (1989)
Bullseye! (1989)
An American Tail: Fievel Goes West (1991) (voice)
Splitting Heirs (1993)
Mary Shelley's Frankenstein (1994)
The Swan Princess (1994)(voice)
The Jungle Book (1994)
The Wind in the Willows (1996)
Fierce Creatures (1997)

With Prince Charles in a scene from a comic video to promote environmental awareness.

'I probably owe my life to the fact that I couldn't get the rest of them to vote for my material. Graham and I wrote this savage attack on the Ayatollah Khomeini, about this frenzied loony with all these religious objections to toilet paper. It was just a scurrilous, way over-the-top attack on Islamic extremists. I thought it was hilarious, and the others didn't, so it never got in. And I owe my life to that, because we would've got at least a fatwah each. Actually, maybe that's what happened to Graham ...'

John Cleese, on writing material for The Meaning of Life

He's an Ex-Python

Cleese has never felt the same emotional attachment to *Monty Python* that some of the other members have, and by 1973 had tired of what the series was doing. He ducked out of the fourth and last series, leaving the five remaining *Python*s to go it alone. His presence – no matter how frustrating or domineering – was sorely missed by the others. They all came to realise that *Monty Python* wasn't just a random collection of talent but a carefully balanced machine that could not operate properly without all of the members. Even so, Palin is on record as saying that, with Cleese's leaving, they all realised how overdomineering he could be. And his departure at least gave Gilliam the opportunity to go in front of the camera more often.

Cleese was now working a great deal with his wife, Connie Booth, and was devoting much time to his newly founded company, Video Arts, which produced training films for companies on a wide range of management issues. After reuniting with the *Python*s to make *Holy Grail* in 1974, Cleese and Booth then embarked on the project that was to seal Cleese's place in the pantheon of comedy – *Fawlty Towers*.

No, You Started It. You Invaded Poland

Basil Fawlty is one of the greatest comic creations of all time, a character very much the product of his maker. His manic, furious inability to cope with even the simplest of life's tribulations lent him an air of deep comic tragedy. The original series contained only six shows, but Cleese and Booth worked tirelessly, crafting every episode, ensuring the internal logic of each was complete and that dialogue and comic

Top: *Cleese in one of his Video Arts training films.*

Above: *Pushed for time in* Clockwise.

timing were perfected. *Fawlty Towers* was more than sitcom: it became an icon of British humour, and is as timeless now as when the first episode was broadcast in 1975. But, as with all gargantuan successes, Cleese lived in the shadow of Basil Fawlty for many years afterwards, emerging from beneath his long pall as man-separate-from-creation only with the success of *A Fish Called Wanda*. What is notable about the discipline and rigour with which Cleese and Booth approached *Fawlty Towers* was that the second series of six was written and filmed four years after the first (1979), and yet they are equal – if not superior – in quality to the first. This was despite the fact that Cleese and Booth had divorced in the interim.

Cleese is very open about his struggle to deal with his anger and irascibility, and in the 70s he underwent a (very un-English) programme of group therapy that changed his life and helped him to understand himself in a way he had never done before. So changed and evangelised was he by the process that in 1983 he published a book, co-authored with his analyst Dr Robin Skynner, entitled *Families and How to Survive Them*, followed a decade later by its sequel *Life and How to Survive It*.

Fishy Business

His work since *Fawlty Towers* has been very prolific in terms of his acting, less so his writing. His film work has been so prodigious (at the last count over 30 films) that for years he added the names of made-up films into his *Who's Who* entry simply to see if anyone would notice (which they didn't). But his biggest post-*Python* success was *A Fish Called Wanda* in 1988. Grossing more than £127 million in box-office receipts, it was the most successful British film of all time until *Four Weddings and a Funeral* came along some years later. Infinitely superior to his previous cinematic venture, *Clockwise*, it established Cleese as a comic force with a new generation of fans, and at long last laid to rest the ghost of Basil Fawlty. The follow-up, *Fierce Creatures* (almost ten years in execution), did not do well at the box office, which was a shame given that it was as accomplished a film as *Wanda*.

Cleese has always been a willing contributor to *Python* events; but, as with all of his work, has tried to distance himself from past victories, choosing instead to focus on future ideas. And he has always been an enthusiastic supporter of his fellow *Pythons*' pet projects, giving of himself when he can. (No one can accuse Cleese of taking too narrow an approach to his work – he's

NAME: John Marwood Cleese
DATE OF BIRTH: 27 October 1939
BIRTHPLACE: Weston-Super-Mare, Somerset, England
SCHOOL: St Peter's Preparatory; Clifton College, Bristol
UNIVERSITY: Downing College, Cambridge University (Law)
MARRIED: Connie Booth (1968–1976); Barbara Trentham (1981–1990); Alyce Faye Eichelberger (1992–)
CHILDREN: Cynthia Caylor (b. 1971 of Connie Booth; played 'Portia Leach' in *A Fish Called Wanda*); Camilla (b. 1984 of Barbara Trentham)
RESIDENCE: London, England; New York

appeared on *The Muppet Show*, in *Cheers*, on *Doctor Who*, as a cowboy in the film *Silverado*, a talking gorilla in *George of the Jungle*, and in Kenneth Branagh's *Frankenstein*, to name only ... er six.) As well as his show-business interests, Cleese is also – for a celebrity at least – high profile with his politics, doing a number of party political broadcasts for the Liberal Democrats and being a vocal supporter of electoral reform in the shape of proportional representation.

All in all, Cleese is without doubt one of this country's most loved and highly respected artists. Bar the odd misjudged advertising campaign, his track record is impeccable and his role in *Monty Python* rightly lauded. Were it not for the Cambridge Footlights, there could well be some legal firm in the City run by the funniest solicitor alive.

Fierce Creatures *(above) and* A Fish called Wanda *(left) used the same cast, but all playing differant characters.*

Books, Records and all Manner of Magnificent Monty Merchandise

The Books of the Films of the TV Series of the Script Meetings of the Curry

They weren't the kinds of books your mum and dad would buy you for Christmas, but they were the kinds of books that kids the country over borrowed from each other with furtive glee and a barely disguised sense of subversion. Because, unlike the TV shows, the *Monty Python* books were downright rude. As a precursor to the immensely popular *Viz* magazine, they used words like 'masturbation' and 'vaginal deodoriser' and carried silly adverts for 'split-crotch football shorts' and devices that stopped 'tiresome ejaculations'. But best of all, they were packed with references to the TV characters, were smothered in Gilliam drawings and contained some fantastically funny compositions, stories and magazine-style columns.

Today, the launch of a book to coincide with a popular TV show is obligatory (as is the launch of a board game, CD-ROM, novelty drinking mug and range of sarcastic birthday cards). But back in the early 70s it was a relatively new phenomenon, and the *Python*s rose to the challenge admirably.

As editor, Eric Idle was most often the driving force behind the books, knocking them into shape and organising the material from the different *Python*s into a cohesive style, but they were still team efforts. Some of them smack of pure commercialism (spot the various compilations and amended reprints) but, by and large, they're all worth having if you're a big fan.

MONTY PYTHON'S BIG RED BOOK
First published 1971
Actually, it's blue, but then what do you expect? *Python*'s first excursion into the world of publishing contained an eclectic mix of material, spanning random compositions to references to many of the popular sketches (including the Poems of Ewan McTeagle, the Piranha Brothers, the Lumberjack Song, the Whizzo Chocolate Assortment, and Silly Walks).

THE BRAND-NEW MONTY PYTHON BOK
First published 1973
More of the same, but this time with less dependency on the TV characters. The hardcover version has a plain white dust jacket with the correct (but spelt wrongly) title. Underneath the actual cover is a saucy photograph of three nude women titled 'Tits 'n Bums: A Weekly Look at Church Architecture'.

THE BRAND-NEW MONTY PYTHON PAPPERBOK
First published 1974
This is exactly the same as the hardback version, but without the false cover and naughty photograph (much to my

adolescent disgust). Memorable for its grubby fingerprints on the cover, this was a real sixth-form-common-room favourite.

MONTY PYTHON AND THE HOLY GRAIL (BOOK)

(also known as MONTY PYTHON'S SECOND FILM: A FIRST DRAFT and MØNTI PYTHØN IK DEN HØLIE GRÄILEN (BØK))

First published 1977

This contains the first and final drafts, production notes, sketches, and photographs (production and off set) for *Monty Python and The Holy Grail*. It is packaged to look like a real production script.

MONTY PYTHON'S THE LIFE OF BRIAN/ MONTYPYTHONSCRAPBOOK

(also known as MONTY PYTHON'S THE LIFE OF BRIAN (OF NAZARETH) and MONTYPYTHONSCRAPBOOKOFBRIANOFNAZARETH

First published 1979

A great addition for fans of *Life of Brian* because it contains the original shooting script (and photographs), which includes scenes later edited from the film. These are (notably) Otto the Jewish Nazi, Pilate's Wife, and a cartoon script of the segment with the shepherds at the beginning of the film, likewise left on the cutting-room floor. It also gives us a glimpse of Cleese's ongoing antagonism with the press, as it details his increasingly irritated correspondence with the *Evening Standard* during production.

MONTY PYTHON'S LIFE OF BRIAN

First published 1979

A small paperback version of the script, including all of the photographs but none of the scrapbook material.

THE CONTRACTUAL OBLIGATION SONGBOOK

First published 1980

'Nuff said.

THE COMPLETE WORKS OF SHAKESPEARE AND MONTY PYTHON: VOLUME ONE – MONTY PYTHON

First published 1981

A compilation of *Big Red Book* and *Brand-New Monty Python Bok* made especially for the UK market.

MONTY PYTHON'S THE MEANING OF LIFE

First published 1983

Similar in style to the *Life of Brian* script of the film, it similarly includes segments later edited from the film (such as 'The Adventures of Martin Luther') and includes many photographs from the Terry Gilliam short film '*The Crimson Permanent Assurance*'.

THE MONTY PYTHON GIFT BOKS

First published 1986

A repackaging of *Monty Python's Big Red Book* and *The Brand New Monty Python Papperbok*, with an additional poster.

MONTY PYTHON'S FLYING CIRCUS: JUST THE WORDS, VOLUME ONE

First published 1989

The complete scripts of the *Flying Circus* television series. Volume one includes episodes 1 through 23, an index and a listing of production and airing dates. Not included are scripts of the animations, which are only mentioned if used as a linking device between sketches.

MONTY PYTHON'S FLYING CIRCUS: JUST THE WORDS, VOLUME TWO

First published 1989

More of the same. Episodes 24 through 45, including an index and listing of production and airing dates.

MONTY PYTHON'S FLYING CIRCUS: JUST THE WORDS

(also known as THE COMPLETE MONTY PYTHON)

First published 1990

Volumes one and two combined together into a regular-sized paperback. Volume two is printed upside down to give the appearance of two front covers. Includes photographs from the television series.

THE FAIRLY INCOMPLETE & RATHER BADLY ILLUSTRATED MONTY PYTHON SONG BOOK

First published 1994

Lyrics and voice scores to virtually all of the Monty Python songs, from the TV series and films. Illustrated with Gilliam's artwork and a photographs from the television series and movies.
 Python and On and On

Epilogue

While I was writing this book, a new, hugely hyped comedy series hit the screens on BBC2. Called *Big Train*, it was – as many pundits predicted – very funny and immediately popular. At the same time, comedian Harry Hill started his new series on Channel Four, and on all channels – satellite and terrestrial – a slew of sketch shows proved once again that the loud bang *Monty Python* made on its arrival is still echoing down the corridors of time. It doesn't take a DNA

test to prove the comedic lineage of the likes of Big Train and Harry Hill, and although both acts are original and funny, they - like so much comedy in the last twenty years - owe an immense debt to Gilliam, Cleese, Palin, Jones, Idle and Chapman.

Today, it is almost impossible to discuss *Monty Python* without every superlative sounding hackneyed or every analysis so far up itself it becomes a *Python* sketch in itself. The *Python*s have long argued that they simply tried to make people laugh, and are slightly incredulous at all the fuss the whole thing has generated. But similar sentiments were echoed by The Beatles ('we were just trying to write some catchy songs,' said Lennon) and it hasn't stopped Revolver being voted the world's favourite album year after year. The public, it seems, will not be denied its legends, and *Python* is unquestionably one of our favourites.

Putting the rather self-effacing modesty of the *Python*s aside, there can be no doubt that *Monty Python*'s Flying Circus changed the nature of comedy forever, or more accurately, changed the nature of comedy more significantly than anyone else since 1969. If the six players had gone on to do nothing else but the work badged 'Python', their place in the Comedy Hall of Fame* would still be secure. That all six made enormously successful solo careers outside of *Python* goes a long way to explaining why, thirty years after the first *Python* show appeared on BBC, I just heard two teenage boys walk past my office window shouting 'I'm Brian and so's my wife'. Now that's immortality.

✱ Mentioned many times in this book, The Comedy Hall of Fame is situated in Basingstoke, just behind the toilets by the station. Admission is free, although you have to ring up in advance so the caretaker can undo the padlock. Take sandwiches.